OFF THE STREETS
AND ON THE
WAY

OFF THE STREETS AND ON THE
WAY

Autobiography *of a*
Former Drug Addict
Now Running a Rehab for Over Thirty Years

Remko Jorritsma

AMBASSADOR INTERNATIONAL
GREENVILLE, SOUTH CAROLINA & BELFAST, NORTHERN IRELAND

www.ambassador-international.com

Off the Streets and On the Way

Autobiography of a Former Drug Addict
©2022 by Remko Jorritsma
All rights reserved

ISBN: 978-1-64960-211-4
eISBN: 978-1-64960-319-7

Cover Design by Hannah Linder Designs
Interior Typesetting by Dentelle Design
Edited by Daphne Self

AMBASSADOR INTERNATIONAL
Emerald House
411 University Ridge, Suite B14
Greenville, SC 29601, USA
www.ambassador-international.com

AMBASSADOR BOOKS
The Mount
2 Woodstock Link
Belfast, BT6 8DD, Northern Ireland, UK
www.ambassadormedia.co.uk

The colophon is a trademark of Ambassador, a Christian publishing company.

TABLE OF CONTENTS

CHAPTER 1

IN NEED OF MONEY

"You grab the envelopes while I keep the door shut," said my brother, while we observed the gas station from the cafeteria.

"All right," I said, turning my head sideways to look at him.

We had hung around together quite a bit lately. Both of us were hooked on heroine and thus always hungry for money. Fred was one in a million. Almost six-and-a-half-feet tall, broad-shouldered, and strong, he was also very handsome. He always had lots of women around him, and I just loved his sense of humor. Although often a bit morbid, it nevertheless cracked me up. In a crowd he was usually the center of attention and often set the mood.

We had a special bond and feeling for one another. His tremendous physical strength, which he wasn't shy to use, gave me a sense of safety whenever we were together. The trouble was that he used that strength against both friend and foe.

That was his big flaw; he always had to have his own way, and whoever opposed him was in for a good smack over the ear. The word *rest* meant nothing to him; he was always up to something, either involved in or on his way to whatever. It was impossible to keep up with him. I always found it enviable that his intriguing character simply opened doors for him which remained closed for others. On the other hand, he often generated aggression in his opponents, so he had to be alert to possible adversaries all the time.

We watched the gas station, and I didn't doubt for a moment that he would keep the door shut once the pump attendant had to fetch something in the back.

My main concern was that someone might spot him while we were on the job because that was the disadvantage of his striking appearance. A vague description was all that the cops would need to know that Fred had been at it again.

Our need for dope was so urgent, we had to score. The minute the pump attendant went into the stockroom to get something, we rushed across the street and went inside. Fred got hold of the doorknob of the stockroom and blocked the doorway, so the attendant couldn't get out. We had checked out the gas station the previous day around six o'clock and had noticed that there were envelopes under the cash box, which we assumed were used to stash away cash.

Nervously, I grabbed in the drawers under the cash box and indeed dug out two fat envelopes. Meanwhile, I heard an enormous bang and the sound of breaking glass. The attendant had smashed the windowpane over the door with an oil can, and glass was scattered all over the place, but Fred stood fast. Like a dart, I dashed through the open door, out of the shop, and disappeared into the maze of neighboring alleys. My condition only allowed me a short run, but that was enough because I didn't notice any sign of pursuit.

Under the cover of a porch, I touched the fat envelopes, and boy did that feel good! I said to myself, "If these are filled with cash, this will be the biggest hit of our lives . . . " Panting, I tore open one of the envelopes. To my horror, all we saw were accounts and coupons—I freaked out!

Fred snatched the other envelope from my hands—this was our last hope—he tore it to shreds . . . Nothing in it either!

"Now I understand why we weren't chased," he hissed, hurling the pile of papers on the pavement.

"I should've made sure and grabbed some money from the cash box," I said. "Now what?" I asked checking the stores. It was late-night shopping.

CHAPTER 2

DAD DROVE LIKE MAD

Dad raced at high speed over the B road from The Hague to De Lier in the Westland area of the Netherlands. He was obviously upset. While moving from the heart of the Schilderswijk in The Hague to our brand-new, single-family dwelling in De Lier, we had taken this route through Naaldwijk many, many times; and we knew the road like the back of our hands. An exciting dream, over and over again. It thrilled me every time we raced by the endless rows of glass hothouses. The blue sky and the sun reflecting in the thousands of windows produced a dazzling dance of light effects. Usually during these rides, you heard a cacophony of my brothers' and sisters' voices, but not this time. Everybody was downcast today. *De Lier was quite an improvement compared to our housing situation in The Hague,* I thought, staring out of the car window.

In the Schilderswijk, an inner-city area of The Hague, we used to sleep in box beds, basically nothing more than old cupboards converted into bunk beds. They were, in fact, big alcoves with doors. Alfred and I slept in the top bed and Rik below. Our oldest and youngest sisters slept in the other cupboards further down the hall. For young people nowadays, this may sound like a hundred years ago; but every week, we were washed in the granite sink under the cold water tap. There you stood, naked, on the cold, kitchen floor tiles, waiting for the wash tub to fill. As we grew older, you could see us, rolled up towels under our arms, walking to the public bath like ducks in a row. The sterile, white, tiled, bare interior of the public bath seemed to me like a sort of converted slaughterhouse. You felt just as naked and cold as stock ready for slaughter. We always tiptoed over the wet floor.

In the coal stove in the living room—the only heating we had in the house—almost all our household refuse was burned in that stove, and the ash man literally only collected ashes. It was common,; nobody ever complained about these things; and it really didn't matter at all. In the wintertime, we enjoyed the cosiness of the burning flames in the stove. Throwing stuff in it ourselves and stirring up the fire was, of course, great fun.

I can still remember the day Dad came home with our very first TV set, a small black and white box—quite a sensation! And the night the *Apollo* landed on the moon; we were allowed to stay up until three in the morning. The playground was the place for playing with tops, marbles, and sometimes new toys—like pea pistols and cross bows.

But the greatest time was the period after Christmas when the hunt for Christmas trees burst forth. The one street had a bitter fight with the other over a Christmas tree—or simply just for the fun of it. We walked around with chains and sticks that we could hardly lift, just as long as it looked dangerous. The rubber catapult was the artillery; but you had to be careful because it was deadly serious, and you could get hurt. The emergency help service was very busy at that time of the year. It could be that your best friend, who just happened to live on another street was suddenly your worst enemy. And if you had fireworks, you were really someone.

Ma bought fireworks at the store, so we always had a supply. When the bazooka came on the market, we had the greatest fun. If you put such a thing in someone's letter box, you mangled a whole doorway, and a bazooka in the exhaust pipe of a car destroyed the whole pipe with an almighty bang. There were cars enough. And then, of course, New Year's Eve itself. The big, brown pan with the rising dough for the "olie bollen," a typical Dutch treat served at New Year's, stood ready on the stove. Our mother, of course, made the most delicious ones in the whole world.

Ma was always sweet to us; we could get away with quite a bit with her, but sometimes we went too far. If anything happened at school, we always said that it was the teacher's fault. And there was regularly something happening because the three brothers were no "angels" just like so many others of our age. One day, we all went to another school.

Our mum was running a store nearby, one that sold cigarettes and all kinds of things. We were allowed to help selling sweets to young customers. In that way, we had access to the sweets but also to the petty cash. I was the youngest brother and probably the last one to begin taking small amounts from the cash drawer. I remember that I was ashamed of myself. At school, we got in with some boys who stole things from shops in town; and at a certain moment, Pa had to come and collect us from the police station because of this. He was very ashamed—and, of course, quite angry—and that meant trouble.

Moreover, Pa was not home very much. He was an interior decorator by training but had had to drop his ambitions in this field for the certainty of a steady income in the civil service. He had to work a lot of overtime in the evening; and if he was home, he always watched some interesting detective film on the TV. That's how I knew him, reading the paper or sitting in front of the TV, while we roamed around the streets. In the neighborhood, there were several notorious families with whom you lived in animosity, without there ever being a real reason to do so. It was just so. You had to be a bit careful. A woman on the second floor was always hanging out of the window and scolding my brother and sister.

"Red pigeon head!" You could hear her yelling throughout the street.

In the summer, we went on vacation to Drente or Friesland. Those were great times, but even greater was a day at the beach. Everybody in The Hague sat together like one lump on the beach on a nice summer day. We regularly did, too. On those days, we left the house incredibly early. One kid sat at the back of Pa on the motor bike, an unsightly DKW, and a second kid sat in front on top of the gas tank. We fought among ourselves to be the one to sit in front on top of the gas tank. It was extremely exciting. The rest of the family took the tram. Equipped with a blanket and a windscreen and your day couldn't go wrong.

Pa always drove fast, but now, he literally raced past any car that happened to appear in front of him. There was a tense atmosphere in the car, and no one said a word. Glumly, I stared out the window at the passing glass hothouses and regular houses on our way to the village of De Lier. Perhaps my parents had realized that growing up in a big city was not good for us and they wanted to make a new start in De Lier.

And their marriage? That was something that up until then, I hadn't paid any attention to. I found De Lier nice. As a kid from the city, there I was suddenly in the middle of market gardeners and farmers, of canals and meadows. In the newly built neighborhood, we were now the wealthy owners of bedrooms and a real bathroom with a shower that had hot water! In De Lier, you could build huts or cars, build a dike in the mud canals, and even try to grow flowers in the backyard.

We roamed around between the hothouses, stole grapes, and chased the pigeons who were brooding. At the baker's, you could get dough to put on your fishing hook; and in the winter, you could skate on the ice, facing into the biting winter wind. Coming home with frozen hands and toes, we thawed out, crying, in front of the central heating stove. In the new neighborhood were many people who had come to live there from The Hague.

Around New Year's Eve, we walked around the village with sticks and whips looking for opponents to fight with over Christmas trees; but De Lier didn't know that tradition, and people looked very surprised at the kids from the city and what they were doing.

Out of boredom, we stole bales of hay out of a nearby farmer's haystack. That certainly created the excitement we needed! The farmer didn't just let us city kids get away with what we were doing. If he caught you dragging a bale of hay off his property, the expression on his face clearly showed what he would like to do—spear you to the ground with his fork. And rightly so. Fortunately, we were quicker and mostly managed to get away.

In order to earn some pocket money, we worked for the market gardener but also sold vegetables door-to-door, which had been dug up to feed the cows. You could earn a decent amount of money from picking tomatoes and lettuce—money that you spent on snacks and things to jazz up your bicycle. I thought it was much better to live in a village than in a city.

Astrid, the eldest, sat still and withdrawn next to me when Pa took the first turning to De Lier. Even Anita, the youngest of us, didn't break the silence in the car, which you could cut with a knife.

For some time now, there had been tension in the family. Especially in the evening, Ma and Pa had disagreements. It began when raised voices could be heard in our bedrooms and the tension in the house kept us from sleeping. Other times, the fights got worse, and they screamed at one another with emotion-filled voices. Sometimes, things were thrown, or we heard our parents crying in despair. At such times, the atmosphere was so tense that all the children, even my two older brothers, burst out in tears. Sometimes, I was so emotional that I didn't know what to do.

It was as if a pair of tongs was pressing together my deepest self and squeezing the tears out. I experienced the bewildering realization that everything which had always been safe, secure, certain, and taken for granted could suddenly become shaky and uncertain. The basis of my very existence shook on its foundations, and fear and uncertainty stared at me like frightening wolves.

Astrid, who was four years older than me, tried to comfort and reassure us, her brothers (of which I was the third in age) and our youngest sister, Anita. Many questions went through my head, in particular, how this would all turn out. My feelings were being hurled back and forth. Sometimes, I toughened up and silently accused my parents for acting so stupidly. At other times, selfish thoughts arose, such as if Pa didn't come home, then we could do more of what we felt like doing! If the arguments quietened down, I quickly tried to forget them and tried to believe that it had all been a bad dream, which was over now and gone forever, and that there was really nothing wrong.

With one last bend in the road, past the baker and a bit of gas to go over the bridge, the ride was over, and we finally got out of the car by our front garden. Relieved, everyone wanted to go to his or her own room to do something else.

Pa decided otherwise and said that before we went off, we should go into the living room. When, with mixed feelings, we were all gathered there, Pa began to explain that things weren't going well between him and Ma and that Ma had left and would probably not return. We heard this with open mouths. Astrid and Anita began to cry.

A SERIOUS TALK

Shocked, we heard that we would have time to decide with whom we wanted to live. Pa talked with each one of us personally. It was the only serious and personal talk that I ever had with my father during my youth. How I wished that, liked other fathers, he would come and cheer for me when I was playing soccer or that he would once come fishing with me, or some such thing—just some personal attention.

Pa was always too busy; his own father had died when he was only three years old, and he had, therefore, missed a fatherly role model in his own youth. Sometimes, he did carpentry work in the shed and made something for the house, and then I respectfully watched his big hands at work. Why didn't those big hands ever lovingly stroke my head?

It was not even a real talk—more an exchange of information. Having been taken aside, Pa explained that I could make a choice.

"Your mother has gone to live with Grandma in Delft," he began. "If you stay with me, then you stay in De Lier; otherwise, you have to move to Delft. You have had time to think about it, and now I would like to hear your answer."

I was nervous also because I didn't know how he would take it, but my choice was determined by my feelings—feelings that longed for Mum. "With Mum" came from the stammering eleven-year-old boy, who sat there perplexed and didn't know how to handle the situation.

"Now that is clear. Then you and your sister will go to your mother, and the rest will stay with me," said Pa, not unemotionally, but nevertheless remaining business like.

So, I moved to my mother's in Delft and lived there for a number of months with Anita, my youngest sister. Again, new school and new surroundings. Less than a year later, without my knowing it, there were new developments. Unexpectedly, we moved back to De Lier. Ma and Pa were going to try to make a go of it again.

It was so good to be with my brothers and sisters once more, although some unbalanced relationships resulted from this. The happiness didn't last long, and again, we were given a choice. I chose for De Lier, rather than for Pa or Ma in this confusing time. The divorce was now definite and irreversible. Fred went with Ma—where they went was not mentioned—and the rest of us stayed with Pa.

Astrid got the much-too-heavy task of caring for all the children. She had to prepare the food and run the household on too little money. As a result of the problems at home and the lack of parental attention, we children were left too much to their own devices. I can remember that in the sixth class I stood in the hall for punishment more than I actually sat in the class. The head teacher obviously had no understanding of my home situation, because he did not make the least attempt to either develope a better relationship with me or to motivate me. Probably, I could not be reached, anyway.

In any event, as a result of missing my lessons, I didn't learn anything, and I didn't even pass the test for admission to high school. The solution for me was a lower administrative economic education and for this school, I had to go to Delft by bicycle. In the meantime, my father developed a relationship with a woman from Wassenaar. It didn't click at all between us, but nevertheless, the marriage went ahead. For us, this was proof of the negative reputation of the fairy tale stepmother. An enemy in the house from whom you couldn't expect anything. Pa was unaware of the fact that she always favored her own children, at least that was our impression. For one reason or another, the house in De Lier was sold, and we moved back to The Hague, somewhere near the Laan van Meerdervoort.

Yet again, another school, another environment. The tension in the house increased daily. As children, we had a sort of feeling of togetherness because of this situation. It was Pa, stepmother, and her children against us. Stepmother used all her tricks to put us in a bad light with Pa. We couldn't speak openly about our own mother. Around that subject, there had developed an atmosphere of taboo, as if it were a hostile element which was best not to mention. In secret meetings, we talked about the injustice and how we could protect ourselves against the power of the "vested order." Also, we asked ourselves now and then how things were going with Ma and Alfred, as we hadn't seen or heard from them for a long time. Running away was a possibility to make another life. During one of the meetings, Astrid said that she had decided to take the step that she had talked about so often. However, she said that she felt rotten about it because she would be letting us down.

The tensions of the past years had become too much for her. Too much was taken, and she had received nothing in return; she was deeply disappointed. I was too young to understand exactly what she meant; she was seventeen. For her, everything had been much more traumatic than for the rest of us.

So Astrid had gone over to the other camp, and really the only question now was who would be the next. I suspected that our stepmother was determined to play it in such a way that eventually we would all walk out. That thought seemed confirmed by the disinterested attitude of Pa toward us. We felt betrayed by him. One evening, I also took the bull by the horns and regarded "the other camp" as a homecoming. Like the prodigal son who was again found, I was welcomed by Mum and also by her friend, Johan, a man, I discovered, on whom you could depend. I also met Alfred, who wanted to be called Fred. Was he ever big! And Astrid—she was living with an American, both of them so full of life. For me, this meant another school and environment. In the meantime, I was finished with puberty and soon discovered the way to the dance clubs. After a year, my brother, Rik, came over to our side, and only my little sister stayed with Pa until his second marriage also failed and she became independent.

In the meantime, my concentration and inner peace, which is so necessary to build up something constructive, was destroyed. By being to so many different schools, I had never been able to develop lasting relationships and never had the feeling that I belonged. I played truant and became a mess. Sometimes, I sat all day in a swimming pool after the swimming lesson was over, looking at the clock until school was done. At home it was cozy. I had my own room and took drum lessons and practiced on them—to the irritation of the neighbors.

Mother and Johan married, and a year, later I got a new little brother. He was a beautiful and healthy baby, and we were all very proud of him. The only problem was that now I had to drastically cut down on my drum practice. It was pleasant to play cards with a case of beer under the table. Weekends, I went to the discos, very clean "soul" places where you had to be dressed in the latest fashion and your hair cut in the current trend. Wearing platform shoes and looking cool, it was a kick vying for the attention of beautiful young ladies.

CHAPTER 3
SPEED

Rob was on leave. He was in the navy for a short enlistment of four years. I met him at a mutual acquaintance's place, and it clicked right away. It was my impression that he was no longer happy being in the navy. Not that it was so bad, and moreover it paid well, but because he was consumed with restlessness. In one way or another, he had to be constantly moving in order to drive away his restlessness. That evening we were going out, before we went into the club, he gave me a shove. "Rem, I have speed with me; do you want a snuff?"

I had heard about speed and had seen people use it.

"I bought a gram through an acquaintance; it's good before going out."

My curiosity was aroused, and I looked eagerly at the paper in which it was wrapped. Rob opened it and with a knife laid out a strip on the palm of his hand and then snuffed it up. Expectantly I looked at his face to see what the result was. "Mmm" was his pleased reaction.

I held my hand out, and he poured a thick line on to it, after which I got it into my nose somewhat clumsily. Immediately, my eyes filled with tears. That stuff hit the lining of my nose so sharply, and that was directly followed by a tingle in my head and a difficult-to-describe change in feelings. I felt as though my senses had gone into overdrive and that I experienced a much more intense feeling for what was taking place in and around me. When I went into the discotheque, it was as if I was completely one with the music, the light effects, and the dancing crowd on the floor.

Certain limits fell away; I moved more freely and was less held back by second thoughts on the dance floor. I had the impression that everyone was friendlier and warmer, the faces prettier and the movements more fluid—as if it were a wonderful play in which everyone had a lead role. We moved on the waves of feeling and rolled along with rhythmic melodies that had been blown over from topical islands.

When the club closed around 1:00 a.m., everyone went home, satisfied with the evening, except Rob and I, who, full of energy and completely insatiable, had the idea that the evening had yet to begin. What an injustice it was to stop such a wonderful dream so abruptly and to send the people out into the cold world. We took the tram to Scheveningen and spent the whole night there; when the last place closed at 5:00 a.m., we walked, still full of energy, back home to Voorburg. With honey in our mouths, we greeted the first people we met who were hurrying to work with sour faces. We talked each other's heads off, without even bothering to listen to one another. We constantly repeated, "Don't talk so much, and moreover, listen." It was irritating in the end.

"Now, I can say it about you with your complaining," I snarled back. The whole night and the following day, we didn't close our eyes. The chattering had finally stopped, but a stream of consciousness remained spinning through our heads. It made me crazy, and in the end, we looked terrible, white as a sheet.

A week later, I longed to again have the kick that speed had given immediately after snuffing. I discounted the disadvantages of the drugs.

After some detective work and making demands on other people, I was taken by an acquaintance to a dealer to buy a gram of speed. We came to an address in the Schilderswijk, and Hans rang the doorbell.

"Just follow me up the stairs," indicated Hans. "If you come with me, he'll know that you're okay."

Above stood a young woman, who watched us critically as we climbed the steep stairs. She was a pretty girl, but she looked tired.

"Just wait here," she told us, meanwhile disappearing through an old, velvet curtain that hung across the living room door. A little later, we heard her voice behind the curtains saying that we could come. In the rather dim living room, there was a TV on in the background.

In a big armchair sat a guy half bent over a living room table. At least three ash trays full of butts and ash stood on the table, which was also littered with all sorts of users' attributes. In the middle was a set of scales. When the guy looked up to see who had come in, I recognized his face. I had seen him more often in the night life. He was certainly no show-off, but he did drive a big American car for the kicks. Probably, he had been a user for a long time.

"Don't just bring people along," he said to Hans. "And don't tell this address further, okay?"

"Okay, why should I?" I replied. He didn't say anything more about it, from which I concluded that he needed the money and perhaps was happy with a new client.

"One gram?"

Hans answered in the positive and with interest looked at how, with a pocketknife, he maneuvered a spoonful of white powder out of a plastic sack and ticked it onto a piece of paper. He put the paper on the scales. It was a bit short, and so he added a knife point.

"It can be a little more," said Hans jokingly.

"Twenty-five guilders, Hans," mumbled the dealer, who had obviously forgotten how to laugh and like, a cheese seller, carefully folded up the package.

Hans paid. "So long, then."

Once outside, we stepped into a doorway in order to divide the gram in half, and we felt confident that we were now assured of a successful weekend.

The speed was not a disappointment. Again, it had the same effect, with a higher dosage, of course, but that was no objection because there was enough. With a gram, you could go through a weekend. The misery was that it took an exceptionally long time to go to sleep, which was pretty exhausting. You needed the Monday and Tuesday to "come to." I no longer visited the childish "soul" place that closed at 1:00 a.m. My new friends all used speed, and the weekend began on Thursday.

One Sunday evening, I again sat on a bus going home. My head felt as light as a balloon that had been blown up too far and was tight from tension. Without being able to stop, I chewed on my lips and tongue and constantly had the feeling that I was being followed. I kept looking around, but I didn't discover any suspicious people. However, the other passengers did keep looking at me. I saw the eyes of the bus driver glaring at me in the mirror. I was an outcast, and everyone was against me. The world was not real; everyone played his sneaky role, and I thought everyone was plotting together to force us into their straight jacket system.

"Station Voorburg" came through the PA voice of the bus driver.

With a disagreeable feeling that all the eyes behind the windows were focused on me, I quickly got off.

"Try to rest a bit," I heard the driver say, as I was walking past his open window.

I looked up and saw a friendly, smiling face. Somewhat embarrassed, I nodded and walked quickly along, but I couldn't stop myself from looking behind me to see if someone else hadn't got off the bus in order to follow me.

CHAPTER 4
NEGATIVE FUTURE

One afternoon, my Dutch teacher had taken me to one side. I had wondered what he wanted. Once we were apart from the class, he looked at me in a friendly way and began to tell me about his own life.

"Look, I had a difficult childhood," he began. "Actually, I have to admit that I made a mess of things in my youth through my own stupidity. But you know how it is. When you're young, you don't care about anything, and you're blind to a lot of things that really are important . . . but, fortunately, everything has turned out well for me. I became a teacher, am happily married, and am enjoying life. So you see, even if things don't turn out so well when you're young, that doesn't mean that your whole life will go wrong." He paused for a minute. "There are always changes," he finished.

I listened to the teacher and didn't know what to say.

I was touched that the teacher gave me special attention, and his words stayed with me. Often, I thought back to that moment and wondered what exactly had moved the man to tell me something so personal. I can only assume that his intentions were good—that was clear. Obviously, there were people who already could see that things were going wrong with me, but they then had a whole other opinion than I did.

If I were to be shaped by the future, then my thoughts went out to all the informative TV documentaries that gave, at great length, statistics about environmental pollution. All the nature films with colorful pictures of the plant and animal world that ended with the tragic announcement that if action is not taken soon, all that beauty is threatened with destruction: pictures of landscapes full of factory pipes whose smoke blot out the sun and the colors of the sky; then the knowledge that a cold war was going on between superpowers, the arms race and the tension that that brought with it.

The developing countries were, in spite of all sorts of well-meaning actions, still places where people suffered from sickness and hunger.

The tropical forests were in a still faster tempo of being cut down. Acid rain, the ozone hole whereby people in New Zealand and Australia could no longer sunbathe without fear of getting skin cancer. Radioactive rays from power stations, but also increasing crime and violence. I saw a world society that was completely gridlocked in a destructive, economic market growth system. A world with enormous political and religious differences whereby each optimistic feeling of hope for something that could turn the tide was smothered. And me? What could I do about it?

I also couldn't do anything that would have any influence on this tragic turn of events. The hippies tried it; they failed, and their ideas disappeared in hash smoke. The world is doomed to a total catastrophe and destruction. No one would be able to live in the completely poisoned and sick biotope of the future was my confirmed conclusion. At a certain time, it would reach the point where human life on the earth's surface would no longer be possible. Perhaps, I fantasized, there would still be rich and influential people who would be realistic enough not to deny the coming catastrophe and make preparations for themselves. They would have had an underground area built with an artificial climate. There they would be protected from all dangerous rays and pollution that made living on the earth's surface impossible because it had been turned into a lifeless chaos by apocalyptic natural disasters.

With many technical aids they could, in any event, stay alive. Walking along the beach in the evening breeze would no longer be possible. And so many other things. As for TV, people would only be able to enjoy the use of videos. Fortunately, there was an extensive video store; but after a while, everything would have been viewed, and the suffocating fact would be realized that nothing new would ever come again. Children would have to see by way of the TV screen how the outside world had once looked—so I fantasized.

At the same time, I thought about the fact that in some lands, people even now were living in sewers. How many children are there in our urban society already who no longer see any real nature or get to enjoy it?

Future? I thought. *What future?*

In my mind, we had perhaps ten years more to go. Therefore, my harsh motto, tinged with Hague sarcasm became, "Have fun, for tomorrow the world will disappear."

I had absolutely no social ambitions. My father had been career-minded and, therefore, had had almost no time for his children. The thought of working forty years just simply to have a gold pen handed over to you by some director or another was, in my eyes, disgusting.

CHAPTER 5

ADRIFT

When I was about sixteen years old, my older sister lived for a time with an American who had been a soldier in Vietnam. She was somewhat on the alternative side and was always coming home with something new. I struggled through the Tibetan *Book of the Dead*, heard about the Aztec culture, and read a lot of semi-philosophical articles in *Bres* because she brought them home. She regularly hitchhiked to Switzerland in order to be in the mountains.

My older brother, Fred, wandered through France with a couple of colorful pals. They played music in order to earn some money, and I think that they also did a lot of other mischievous things to keep themselves alive. In any event, every few months, he came home with much gusto, wild stories, and exotic friends in order to get rested up a bit. Ma had to make pancakes for his friends and wash and mend their clothes. Johan took the playing cards out of the cupboard and made sure that there was a crate of beer under the table. Fred demanded a lot. But you could always have a great laugh with him, and that made up for a lot.

During the summer vacation before my final year in school, I heard that Fred was in Paris. Paris—that struck me as being a challenge. My mother gave me the addresses of Fred's girlfriends in Paris. My eternal problem was money—I didn't have any. In a search through my room, with much difficulty, I put together two guilders and fifty cents. Nonchalance and a craving for adventure won out over my common sense, and so I started out.

I left a short note behind. "I'm visiting Fred in Paris . . ."

The cheapest and quickest way to travel was to hitchhike. En route, it soon appeared that fortunately I was not the only one who couldn't afford an interrail ticket and was trying to hitchhike. At every important intersection, there was a group of young people looking for a lift. Proletarian travel. That gave a youth cult atmosphere. People coming from all directions met each other in the noise of the flashing tin idols of the twentieth century. Meetings were casual—often just a hello—and, sometimes, hitchhiking for a while with one another, regular socially critical discussions, and a good bit of fooling around.

I was sixteen, open to everything, but had no idea what "everything" meant exactly. The hitchhiking went well, and I slept that night somewhere under the sky just on the ground a bit away from the highway. The following day, I got a lift in a fast BMW. Maybe the driver was trying to impress me because he rode like crazy. When we came to the outskirts of Paris, I was excited by the impressive road network. Then suddenly, the car door was opened, and I had to get out.

There I was in the big city. I have been to Paris many times since, and each time, I again experience the beauty of the architecture as real excitement. It is a city with allure and rich culture. Amsterdam and Prague also give me that same feeling of excitement. Impressive architecture can still fill me with wonder as I walk through the classical cities of Europe.

Lugging my knapsack, I wandered tirelessly through the city in search of the street where, according to the information I had, my brother could be found. Just as great an experience as the city itself were the distances between metro stations. I couldn't change my two guilders fifty, and so I had extra pleasure on the metro because I was forced to make free use of it. It was boiling hot, but the French make sure no one need suffer from thirst, as everywhere there are small fountains with fresh water. After a lot of hand gestures and often walking in the wrong direction, around about twilight, I saw a street sign that had the same name as that written on my piece of paper.

Eventually, I came to a doorway that led to an inner courtyard. This was it. I knocked and called out; and after a while someone came who, after looking at my paper, nodded but then went away.

After another while, a middle-aged lady came toward me talking in what, for me, was not understandable French. I tried to communicate and could make out that Fred had indeed been at this address but that he had already left.

"Nice, Nice," the woman repeated, pointing to a parked car. "Hm, so he has gone to Nice," I concluded. *But that doesn't help me*, I thought.

I hoped to be invited to spend the night and tried to explain that I was Fred's brother. But that didn't lead to the desired result. "Nice, Nice," she repeated, looking toward the street with her big, brown eyes.

She doesn't understand that it's late, I thought. French hospitality did not extend to an invitation for a drink; I had always heard that French wine was the best in the world and that in its country of origin, it was liberally offered, but not that evening, not for Remko.

At a certain point, the woman apparently found that the "conversation" had lasted long enough, and she abruptly turned around and left.

Still a bit bewildered, I stood there as the woman disappeared from sight. This I hadn't counted on, and I even felt a tear of loneliness well up, but I controlled myself.

"Nice?" I had heard Fred speak about it. Many young people who slept on the beach, the Mediterranean Sea—it all sounded good. I could suddenly feel the tiredness of the day in my body. I looked for a protected place in a kind of doorway and quickly fell asleep, cozy in my sleeping bag. I woke up sweating in the middle of the day. My muscles were stiff, and I splashed water on my wrinkled face at one of the fountains in order to straighten it out. *Paris*, I thought as I stretched, *and soon Nice*.

I already imagined myself laying on the beach enjoying myself, and with renewed inspiration, I went by metro to the road that led to Lyon.

At that road, more than fifty people were standing, waiting for a lift. When I asked someone how long it took to get a ride, he just got a lift and pulled me into the car with him.

"You're lucky; sometimes, it takes hours before you get away from here."

"A Hollander," I said happily surprised.

"How did you guess?" was his dry reply.

I had had luck getting away so quickly, but our lift was a Citroen 2 CV, whose back seat had been taken out, so that we sat on the uncovered metal bottom. The thing went fifty miles at the most, and we got a numb bottom from that metal floor because the car wobbled about like jelly.

"Doesn't matter," said my partner, "as long as we get out of Paris because further up is better for hitching a ride." At the same time, he gave me a piece of bread with vegetables on it.

"Thanks, where are you going?" I asked. I ate the bread like it was cake.

"Lyon," he said.

"Now, let's see who is the first then," I challenged him.

"That will certainly be you because you're still young, and that's what counts," he prophesied. "But I'm not in a hurry," he assured me.

Later that morning, the car took another direction, and so we hitched from the turnoff. We didn't stand next to each other because then it's easier to get a lift. This happened quickly, and when evening came, I found a spot in the open air to spend the night. After another long day of hitchhiking, I arrived in Marseilles and decided to go directly to the harbor and find a place to sleep by the sea. I wanted to see the Mediterranean Sea, and with renewed energy, I hurried on.

When I came through a working-class neighborhood and was walking past a cafe, I was suddenly stopped by a couple of guys who began to pull on my jacket.

"Hey, hey, relax," I said defensively.

The gentlemen looked quite ruthless, and I understood that they wanted to buy my leather jacket. One of them pushed a bill of twenty francs in my hands. My leather jacket was worth much more, but their threatening behavior convinced me that I should accept the offered price. In my shirtsleeves, I went on further and at last came to the harbor. Someone was sitting on a stoop eating French bread. He looked like a traveler like me, and so I went and sat beside him. I could use a bit of company.

"Where are you from?"

"Germany." Oh, a German. Spontaneously, he gave me a portion of his bread.

"Do you know a hostel somewhere around here?" I asked, pretending I could pay for it.

"Expensive," he said meaningfully. "I know a building," he said laughing. It soon appeared that he had found a good place where I could spend the night. In this case, it was a house under construction right by the sea.

A soft breeze was blowing from the sea, bringing with it a new smell from the water. The following day, I sat for hours looking at the deep blue water. It was a great sight to look at the restless sea crash against massive rocks. It soon made me forget the loss of my jacket. I could imagine that this beautiful panorama had inspired many writers to produce poetry. Fishermen who, to my mind, were catching only small fish and the local youth who daringly and skillfully dove into the cool water from the rocks completed this paradise-like picture.

The German was also on his way through, knocking about to see more of the world, just like I was. The second similarity between us was that he had just as little money as I did. He suggested that we take a room for a week in a four-star hotel and then run out on the third night. That plan was too daring for me; I had no desire to meet up with a French cop. But the problem of an empty stomach was there, and we couldn't ignore it. Tourists were everywhere, and their eating habits on the terraces and in restaurants struck us by the fact that, in principle, we couldn't even buy a chewing gumball. Contrary to the beauty of nature and the purity of the bright blue water, we polluted our spirits with thoughts about how to get some money.

Eventually, we stole from several tourists and could quiet our stomachs. After a few days, I went on to the beautiful sea resort, Nice. Here, many young people had also gathered to enjoy the beautiful sea and beach. Many slept on the beach, and actually there was a whole beach culture. Soon, I had contact with a Dutchman and joined in the fun and games. On the beach, there were also Englishmen who kept themselves apart from the others. They had whole mobile kitchens with them and regularly cooked their eggs, ate their soup, and drank their tea at set times.

You could earn a few cents if you sold ice cream for beach restaurants. Others who had the talent for it spent their time entertaining, such as playing music, fire-eating, or making chalk drawings on the boulevard. An attractive option was to just try to make up to a girl with money. Many literally took a grain from the overwhelming richness that was spread out before the tourists and the French themselves. Never had I seen such enormous battleships of pleasure yachts, as well as Porches, Mercedes, and other expensive things. My acquaintance fortunately had some money, and at the end of market day in the city, there was enough fruit lying around to fill up on. Hanging around suited me well, and the weather was exceptional. Mornings waking up on the beach and then taking a refreshing dip in the sea . . .

In the couple of weeks that I stayed there, I met a lot of people, but no Fred. I asked people who were on the move if they knew my brother. That was not so strange because he was so conspicuous that wherever he went, most people remembered "Red" very well, either in a negative or a positive sense. After a couple of weeks, I thought that it was time to go home, but I didn't look forward at all to hitchhiking the whole distance.

"Why don't you just go to the consulate?" asked an acquaintance on the beach.

"What do you mean?" I asked.

"Now, the Netherlands consulate here in Nice—if your money is, so to speak, stolen—they lend you money for your return trip—it's simple."

"What a good idea," I replied and immediately left. I thought that I had been away long enough, and I hoped that with the money I would borrow, I could take a train home.

In the deluxe consulate building, I gave the standard story to a well-groomed Netherlands lady.

"I don't have a red cent left, and next week, I have to go back to school," I explained.

"So everything was stolen, and you really have nothing left?" she asked while taking a questionnaire out of the drawer under the counter.

"Everything," I replied.

"What is your name?" she asked. I told her. "What, do you have a brother with red hair?" she asked indignantly.

"Uh, yeah. Why, do you know him?" I answered with surprise.

"Yes, we know him; you won't get five cents from us," she said suddenly in coarse Dutch, while taking back the questionnaire from where she had just pulled it out.

"How come?" I stuttered.

"Because on several occasions, money has been loaned to your family, and it has never been paid back," she said disapprovingly, and I could see from her face that I could forget this possibility. When a minute later, I found myself outside the door, I sat down on the stoop in front of the consulate, feeling totally defeated.

I realized that I would have to accept that I must make the whole trip back to The Hague without a cent. That idea was suddenly too much. I was overwhelmed with a feeling of loneliness and couldn't hold back a few tears. What had I begun? *Long live fun! Yeah, yeah—so much fun, it wasn't any more,* I whimpered to myself. A bit of "freaking out" here, a bit there. I saw it all as black, there on that stoop, until suddenly someone bent over me. It was a woman, and her hair fell over me like a beautiful coat.

"Here, go home quickly," she said in clear Dutch, and I looked with surprise at the two hundred francs she put into my hand. Before I could turn around to see her, she was gone, but I knew that it must be the woman from the consulate. Maybe she had seen this teenager go outside and—defeated—go and sit on the stoop.

Had she been moved by pity? Surprised, I looked once more toward the entrance to the consulate, but there was no one to be seen. In one blow, I felt rich, and my sentimental mood disappeared—what a bit of money can sometimes do. The money, however, was not enough for the whole train ticket from Nice to the Netherlands, so I kept some of it apart to be able to take the train from Paris home.

When I found the hitchhiking spot to begin the trip to Paris, five weeks had already passed. I went via "Napoleon's route" back to Paris. Amazing how the enormous armies of Napoleon could make their way through the rough and steep mountainous terrain and over the small, crooked roads through the mountains, while I let myself be driven over the road. Despite a couple of good lifts from truck drivers, it took a couple of days to get to Paris. I arrived exhausted. The typical smells of the city did me good, and as it was early, I went by metro first to have a look at the Eiffel Tower and then Notre Dame before finally going to the Gare du Nord. At the station, I found out that I was too late for the intercity train to Amsterdam, which meant that I would therefore have to wait several hours and even spend the night there. As I was very tired, I took things as they came and settled myself on a bench and tried to get some sleep. Hours went by, but because of the noise and busyness of the station, I couldn't sleep.

A man came and sat next to me and asked me something I couldn't understand until he switched to English. After I had told him how long I had to wait, he assured me in a fatherly way that it was dangerous to spend the night in the station and offered me a place to sleep. Naively, I thought that he was referring to a sort of youth hostel. After some doubt, the feeling of hunger and great tiredness led me to accept the invitation. On the way, the man bought something for me to eat. The concern that he had was good, but his motives were certainly not.

Once in his house, it seemed as if paralysis came over me, which I could barely resist. The following day, I was ashamed of myself that I had allowed this to happen. I asked myself what had so paralyzed me and was angry with myself. I pushed away the thought of what had happened; and with time, it quickly faded, but a certain dislike of people with this kind of appetite was implanted in me.

It was good to finally sit in the train. It was full of young people who were going back to the Netherlands from vacation, and there was a lively atmosphere and a lot of chattering.

After many hours, we rolled into The Hague, and I saw the run-down but oh-so-well-known houses on the Parallelweg in front of the station as we passed by.

"Couldn't you even have said goodbye?" asked my mother, annoyed but happy to see me again.

"Sorry, Mum," I said, with a happy expression, and it felt so good to be able to give my faithful mother a hug again.

RECKLESSNESS

A couple of years later, when I was eighteen, I had the chance to buy an old motorcycle, a Suzuki 500 cc.

While several acquaintances stood watching in a doorway, I came riding up and turned the gas up to make an impression. However, the strength that was discharged was so great that the thing flew out from under me and lurched along muchfurther. While my public doubled up laughing, I sat with a painful behind on the street.

My right leg was cut open after I had fallen flat on a gravel path. Probably, the cycle had a crooked frame because once when I took a very sharp curve via an emergency exit onto the highway, the backside and the back wheel began to shake and slip. I got quite a shock, but with some effort, I was able to keep the flying monster under control. I realized that riding a motorcycle was not my calling.

Four wheels under me made me feel safer. The first car I bought cost less than two hundred guilders. I didn't have a driving license nor insurance and had not even had any driving lessons.

My brother, Rik, had given me some instructions. "Just push down on the accelerator, let it go, push in the clutch if you have to shift and steer—that's all," he instructed me.

"And braking?" I asked.

"As little as possible," he said with a grin.

I had watched how it was done when I had been in a car with someone else.

I decided to just begin practicing by driving through the city. Someone from the right, who I thought should stop, just drove on—bang!

My front right fender was bent. I saw the wronged driver stop on the other side of the road. My impulsive reaction was to step on the gas and get away from there. Swearing, I accused myself for not having driven slower and more carefully. I quickly drove to Scheveningen and saw in my mirror that fortunately there was no trace of the police and no other signs that I was being followed. Somewhat relieved, I quickly went into a parking lot in Scheveningen to get my breath and to examine the damage.

In the lot, I tried to back up between two other cars, like a racing car driver does. While I was doing that, a sharp tearing sound made me step on the brakes. Then I saw that I had misjudged the angle of turning, for when I jumped out of the car to take a look, I saw to my horror that the bumper of the parked car had been pushed into my back fender. Swearing, I got back behind the steering wheel and freed the car with a grating sound from this position and raced back to the junk yard in my neighborhood. The amount I got for the wreck was twenty-five guilders.

At least it's better than riding around in such a dented thing and getting caught, I thought.

CONSPICUOUS

The first ride was typical for the rest of my participation in car traffic. Every time I bought a jalopy, I drove carefully and didn't have any accidents, but the curse followed me like a hungry bloodhound, and every so often, I again drove a car to total loss. Then I had to step on the accelerator and sometimes came to the junkyard with smoking tires from the rubbing of the wheels against the fender, to turn in the wreck for a few guilders. Fortunately, there were no injuries. Because I often drove at night for entertainment, I was regularly stopped and heavily fined.

KNIFE

Going out was the great pleasure of my life. I looked forward to the weekend like a hungry lion eyes a zebra. Fortunately, my weekend began early in the week on Wednesday night. This was because the place where I went opened then. I regularly had girlfriends, but I didn't feel any responsibility toward them, and I never had serious intentions. It was just for the time being. Something had to be going on—crazy music for dancing, meeting up with an acquaintance, going to the movies, or getting a kick from taking drugs. I wasn't aware of any eventual results, and it didn't even occur to me to think about it. I worked for temporary employment agencies in different jobs. Friday was pay day, and we earned well in those days. We bought new clothes in town, paid some debts to the drug dealers, and scored a fresh package of speed and got a kick!

Scheveningen was my going-out mecca. That evening was as usual. Early on, hanging around in The Paard, sometimes there was a reasonable rock band, but mostly it was rubbish. Then to Hans and Gretel in Scheveningen. In that club, they played the current pop music, and there was an atmosphere that you could get addicted to. There, everyone met each other; and when at 3:00 a.m. the fluorescent lights went on—which was the only effective way of getting guests to leave—everyone hated it. Some of the vainer people made sure that they had left before the fluorescent lights were turned on, as they preferred not to be seen in such a bright light.

Closing time was tiresome, as if you were shaken awake out of a nice dream, but the real night freaks went on to the "Warehouse," which was open until 5:00 a.m. If you had been taking speed, you still had enough energy; and after that time, it was mainly the users that you met up with.

After The Warehouse, there were places where you could go to until 10:00 a.m. But around that time, the atmosphere had dropped to zero; and by then, you mostly just met up with criminals, prostitutes, junkies, dealers, transvestites, and other lost souls drunk, stoned, or on speed.

One evening, I was in the Warehouse sitting in a corner by the dance floor. You could always find me there by the dance floor, almost never at the bar. The place was half-full of obscure characters and a couple of well-known ones, among them my brother.

"He, Pee Wee, move over," hissed a guy, pushing me aside.

"Relax, man," I answered, whereby he stared at me with a face full of anger and threatened me by saying that I should keep my mouth shut.

"Had a bad evening or something?" I tried to say something that might cool down the situation, but the guy had a hard head and was like a bull storming its way around the arena with two spears in its neck. To my relief, at that moment, the doorman came between us and directed the bull to the door in order to throw him out of the club.

"I'll be waiting for you," hissed the bull as he made for the door.

Maybe the doorman took my side because I knew him. It was about 4:00 a.m., so I forgot the incident and didn't take the threat seriously. When I finally came outside, along with my brother and another friend, there indeed were my two pals in the doorway, waiting for me. I wasn't a fighter, but this time, there was nothing else to do. It was as if a light was turned out the atmosphere in the doorway changed so fast. I felt an enormous aggression well up within me, and everything happened very fast. Too fast. I can't remember if I gave the bull a kick or if it was one of his cronies.

Everyone got into the fight, and hard blows were exchanged. At a certain time, I got a hard push against my back, and then perhaps a few more here and there; but at such a time, there was no realization of pain. We were probably getting the upper hand because at a certain point in, they began to retreat. They realized their forthcoming defeat and therefore suddenly rushed away from the Gevers Deynoot Plein in front of the Kurhuis. We ran after them in order to satisfy the anger that they had aroused in us. Halfway over the street, I was surprised to discover that my back was wet. Still running, I quickly rubbed my back and saw, to my amazement, that my hand was covered in blood. A few seconds later, everything turned black, and I passed out.

That night, I woke up in the intensive care unit of a hospital. I was buckled to the bed, and I saw here and there infusion needles and tubes. The nurse was right next to me. She looked at me, with her deep blue eyes, frowning.

"Hello, we have everything under control; you don't need to be afraid," were her first words. I was speechless but felt a searing pain near my lungs. "Just lie as quietly as possible and try to relax," said the nurse.

"What happened?" I asked.

"You've been stabbed in the back with a knife, and you're lucky that it was your lung and not your heart that was punctured."

The second night in intensive care, I woke up because of noise. When I looked around to see where it was coming from, I saw that my elderly neighbor, who was completely tied up, was trying to pull the infuse and the catheter out of his body. I saw from the pained face of the man that he had had enough. Shocked, I looked at the place where the nurses tended to sit, but they were already on their way. I pretended to sleep and saw how the man was again "laid down" with great effort by the nurses and knocked out with an injection.

What a world, I thought.

After a couple of days, I was allowed to go to the conversation room, which was full of acquaintances, and of course, Fred, all in good spirits, there to encourage me. It pleased me that all the guys had come to visit me.

"Hey, mate," Fred said, "I had to look through photos down at the police station to try and identify the guys who did it, but they weren't among them. Having said that, don't you worry, I didn't see your photo there either, but I did see a couple of other photos of people who are standing right here with us." Everyone laughed.

"That's a great comfort to me; it sure makes me feel safe," I went along with him.

"And look, just for you," he continued, and someone placed a large flowerpot on the floor next to my bed. Later, it appeared that they had just picked up the flowerpot from somewhere in the hall of the hospital. But that didn't detract from the good intentions that were behind it. I had a good laugh; it was just like them to do something like that.

WAR

In the hospital, I had a lot of time to think about things, but my thoughts gave me no peace. *Who stabs a person in the back with a knife for no reason? I didn't even know the guy.*

"Everywhere, there's war," I concluded after watching the news on TV. "Was it ever different?"

During this time, I came to understand that, in fact, war is being waged everywhere. Not only military wars here and there in the world but war on all levels and fronts. The man next to me in Intensive Care fought for his own life; competing businesses wage war to get customers and to increase their profits. To get money, people bash each other's heads in. There is war in politics to get power. Drug wars, spiritual wars, ideological wars, and wars within families. There are boundaries; and everywhere and when these boundaries are crossed, tensions arise.

I suddenly realized that almost every piece of this world was taken. In the Netherlands, it can be clearly seen because there is no ground to be found which wasn't fenced in. No piece that didn't have an owner. Even the surface of the water was owned, and you could fish only if you first paid for a license. Yes, the beach still belonged to everyone, although sometimes it was so crowded that you literally had to conquer a piece of it to be able to sit quietly. My parents used to do that by getting up very early and then staking out a space with wind screens and beach chairs.

Battles rage between religions, races, and nationalities for a better social position. Every battle has its own particular weapons, I philosophized.

I didn't have a goal to strive for, at any rate. I didn't strive; I existed and tried to enjoy life. Why? Probably because everyone else seemed to be striving to reach a particular goal, and I had none. I looked for kicks, and the kicks themselves were the goal. Was it my Western mind that said that this was not a goal in itself? It was said that the African only works if his money had gone or if there was no more fruit left to eat on the tree.

Only then, if it was really necessary, was work called for. According to the African, work was hunting, and that, at least, was pleasant "work." My father worked so that he could take early retirement and enjoy the freedom that went with it and the permanent pension. But by then, you were already getting on in years. Why should you wait so long and sweat so hard to fill the present, with your eye only on enjoyment sometime in the future? Was today not looked down upon because it only served the future? And who knew what the future would bring? How many people had a heart attack from that hard work and then didn't enjoy one cent of their pension? On the street, there is strife, even in the club, just between young people. There were always fights and incidents or ordinary people who just didn't like each other on first sight. From childhood on, my sister was pestered because she had red hair. Does a person, because of the emptiness of his own ego, find it necessary to humiliate others in order to give himself a feeling of identity? If you triumph over others, does that make you someone? In sports, this underlying motive is sometimes clearly depicted. The numero uno was honored, mentioned, rewarded, but above all, received publicity. Winning made the name known, and if that happened, then were you someone? With the name came the pride. Pride raised you above others. The exalted pharaohs were afflicted with that kind of contempt; they abused thousands of people in order to have a pyramid built for themselves in order to attain an eternal name. Was the unnamed slave less that Ramses himself? In fact, a despicable situation.

The winners were someone; the losers were not. They felt inferior in comparison to their "superiors." Mentally and physically handicapped persons were still more or less considered "inferior." When we saw them participating at the Paralympics, it was often, for some, a reason to laugh. Adolph Hitler murdered them. At present, we are heading in the direction where medical advice is to have an abortion if it is even suspected that there is a "defect" in the fetus.

Still, everyone is afflicted with aggression. Why and who has put it in us?

Are we born in order to strive? Are we falling into traps and fighting the wrong battle? There are people who fight for the preservation of the environment. And that's good, but then why do they themselves ride in cars and pollute just as much as others do? It's a good fight, though, for the environment, but a lost cause in my opinion. Political divisions and interests will always be a barrier for an effective fight against environmental pollution. The economic growth market system stands in the way. Marx rightly opposed capitalism, but look at what misery communism has caused.

Self-justification and deadening one's own conscience or simply for advertising purposes are often the underlying motives of rich westerners for sponsoring help organizations. Were there also people who had a genuine desire in their hearts, without any ulterior motive, who put all that they had into the fight against need? I hadn't met up with them. Still, I maintain that this combativeness does exist in people in order to fight the good fight.

However, I was not able to do this because of all my addictions.

Addiction meant, in the long run, that you had lost the power over yourself and were constantly forced to repeat certain things. In my case, it was drugs with all the consequential results. Even if I would try to think differently and set another goal for myself—a beneficial goal, of course—then I was still not able to attain it. *What would be a good battle to fight?* I asked myself. To have a faithful marriage, to keep relationships, and to ensure a home for the children. Perhaps the most difficult battles there are. I thought that I had made a whole new discovery through these reflections.

My parents were divorced, so they hadn't succeeded. How could I hope to succeed if, at my age, I was already unable to maintain any sort of relationship? I would never succeed unless something very radical were to happen.

Since I couldn't foresee anything that would be likely to change this situation. These reflections didn't bring about any rest or peace in me, so I had to move back to my old life philosophy again—to be able to find relaxation; long live fun!

Now? Yeah, forget it, the world is already too complicated. I'll see what happens, I thought, which meant, in fact, that I stayed on the same track which I was already on.

Actually, I was off the track, but not yet out of it all because I was certainly not tired of life, and you never knew what the future might bring. That thought gave me rest and hope. It was only that this was such a long trail, so again I just dreamed it away.

CHAPTER 6
HEROINE

It was always busy in the club. The rhythmic rock that was carefully chosen by the disc jockey, without commentary between records, created the special atmosphere of my favorite place to go to in the evenings. The central point was the dance floor that appeared to move due to the light effects, around which were located different bars and places to sit. The colorful public were dressed, in general, according to the mode of the moment. Speed, which can be likened to ecstasy, was the popular drug, along with alcohol. Those who had the financial means treated themselves to cocaine. There were regular dealers who could, with the agreement of the doorman, carry on their business, although there was always an atmosphere of secretiveness and watchfulness. The "big dealer" used middlemen to cover for him.

One particular dealer was well-regarded. He had money and drugs. We users had either money or drugs; in other words, when we came, we had money, during the evening, drugs, and at the end of the evening, nothing more. In the long run, the club owners, dealers, and doormen were usually rich, unless something unexpected happened, and that was sometimes the case. A doorman had to always be on his guard against reprisals from guests for having been thrown out of the club for one reason or another. Dealers could themselves become addicted, ripped off, or picked up by the narcotics squad. Now and then, there were fights. Women were often the reason for much mischief. The changing contacts within the scene didn't help much for mutual understanding. There were also times when people whispered in each other's ear that it would be advisable to get an antibiotic cure from the doctor because venereal disease was going around.

Tourists who came to buy drugs were put off in all possible ways and made fools of. There was a lot of dried cow manure sold as hash or soap powder for cocaine.

"They can drop dead," was the motto.

I was usually soon broke. How could I ever suspect that, along with my treasurer, I would one day buy a house from this very same club owner to use as a recovery/rehabilitation center. Life can certainly be strange! One evening, a Chinese man was there. I had seen the guy before, and I had wondered what he was doing. He inhaled through a tube the smoke from a powder which was on silver foil and heated up with a cigarette lighter. The whole operation seemed strange to me and gave me a creepy feeling, as if he were busy putting pure poison into his body.

That's something that I'll never begin with, I thought. It was the middle of winter.

"Rem, can you help me move this coming week?" asked an acquaintance.

"Sure, but then you'll arrange something?" I hinted.

"Hey, you know me," he answered meaningfully. A couple of days later, we wormed our way through the snow in a little car about the size of a cookie jar.

"You've found a great room, Chang, right in the middle of town," I complimented him. "Yeah, and right close by everything."

After fooling around a while and a lot of laughs, my toes began to feel frozen. This wouldn't have happened if I hadn't had on white, patent leather shoes with pointed toes—the latest fashion—or if Chang hadn't offered a smoke as a warmer-upper.

"I have skat; that makes you feel good and warm," he said, sitting at a table and taking the stuff out of his pocket. With great precision, he unfolded a paper as if there were gold in it. It was a whole ritual, in which a mirror, a knife, and a snuff pipe were used. The brown pellets were finely chopped and sifted in a line across the mirror.

"Is this the warmer-upper?" I asked him and watched expectantly how he snuffed up the strip with the tube.

I couldn't resist when he pushed the mirror toward me, on which a new strip of brown powder had been sifted. I didn't even ask what it was but quickly snuffed the powder and soon experienced that my expectations had been met. It was nice and warm inside and felt good and light. Later, I fell asleep and had a good rest. I liked it better than speed, and the next day, I hurried over to my friend to ask where I could buy skat.

"You can get it from me," he told me honestly, " but . . . just so that I won't be blamed later after you've become addicted, I want to tell you truthfully . . . it's heroine."

I was shocked. "Heroine is dangerous," I blurted out.

"You have to keep it in hand, control policy," he replied, as if that were a natural thing for him.

Keep it in hand, I thought. *Yeah, I did that, in fact, with speed*, I reasoned. "With speed, you can't sleep, and in the end, you're crazy as a loon. With that stuff, I slept well, so what's really worse? I can keep it in hand," I said self-confidently, but in the back of my mind, there was a big question mark. That day, I was, in fact, really stoned, and I was already addicted.

One disadvantage I soon discovered; the stuff was more expensive than speed, and moreover, it was more quickly consumed. While originally, I was emotionally addicted to speed, I soon realized another great disadvantage of skat; it was not only emotionally addictive, but within a couple of weeks of first using it, I also began to feel physically rotten when I woke up in the morning. The first thing I wanted and thought about was skat—I had to have it! Despite using it, I still managed to do administrative work via employment agencies.

MA BELIEVES

At a certain time, my mother was converted to Christianity which, in fact, she certainly didn't hide from public view. A couple of years before that, the same thing had happened to my oldest sister. They preached at me and urged me to read a bunch of books. However, I saw how they had both changed before my eyes, although they still went through a long period of depression and difficulties. I had nothing against the faith, but I just didn't see how it could help me. I didn't have any belief in it. What could I do with a belief that was full of commandments and laws that I couldn't keep?

Amongst the literature that I was given was a good book entitled, *The Planet Called Earth*, that told about the end of time.

Now, my future wasn't so rosy, so could I also take this on board—"the end of time!" Those are loaded words!

Still, the book gripped me, and I read about a future scenario, which the author declared was based on biblical data and prophecies. Military campaigns from the future "third world war," political developments from just before the last terrible war, and a world religion encompassing all religions, over which a false messiah would rule. Occult influences and disgusting immorality and crime would greatly increase and mislead many people, cause them traumatic fears, and ultimately destroy them. It would be an "hour" of complete satanic rule when evil would appear at its worst.

In the chaos of that time, people would rise up against each other, and there would be great fear. Still, the message of Christ, which said that He would win over evil through the forgiveness of sins even in this apocalyptic period, would be spread throughout the entire world. Even angels would become visible in that time and take part in spreading the message of Christ. Then, at a time when if there were no end to the destruction, no man would survive, Christ would return to the world to save it from Satan and all his dictators, according to the book. A judgment throne would be set up, and every person would be made responsible for his own deeds. Those who had done evil would reap evil for eternity.

Then the so-called thousand-year kingdom of peace would be established. In that kingdom, peace would reign over the whole planet, and nature would be restored. People would respect the law of God and multiply. The words of the Bible—"their swords will be made into plowshares"—would be fulfilled. Right would triumph; children could again quietly play; and those who accepted the Word and turned to God would be given everlasting life.

The biblical words were brought into relationship with actual events and developments occurring in our century, and I must admit that this led to some interesting conclusions which seemed very real.

With this information in mind, my perspective on many newspaper articles became much broader.

LIVING IN A ROOM

Fred had rented a room in a ritzy house in the Archipel neighborhood of The Hague. All the rooms in the house were rented, and most of them were lived in by students. I was looking for a room, and when one came free, I was tipped off about it. Fred made a copy of the front door key, and I moved in before I had even seen the caretaker.

"I haven't paid any rent for three months, and I haven't heard anything," Fred confessed, slapping me on the shoulder.

"This is great." The room I moved into was very spacious—at least forty-five feet long—with five big windows looking out on the shopping street below.

The lovely classical house gave off a sort of royal feeling. I quickly moved in with all my belongings, including my drums, to the irritation of my fellow tenants. My girlfriend was sixteen and regularly came over after school in order to share my kingdom with me. We had fun. In the meantime, the money that I earned from my job was spent much too quickly, and I was forced, along with other friends, to resort to taking some of the dairy product deliveries, which were left in front of the store just across the street at five o'clock in the morning. We literally kept ourselves alive with those fruit yogurts and puddings.

The students living around us began to disappear, one after the other. Probably because of the trouble we caused. We rented the rooms they left behind to destitute people looking for a place to live whom we met in the clubs. In the drug sub-culture, there is an expression that "everyone knows everyone." People knew one another. Like a shock wave, news also went through the drug scene. Everyone was sad about death announcements. Ferry was a good-looking dynamic guy, who was always well-groomed, had been to a good school, and was only just twenty years old. Ready for the future, ready to live and to take part in society. And now a funeral, dead? No, that couldn't be—such a lively guy! Was it really true? But it was true.

The family must have been completely shattered. He had taken different drugs at one take, and the combination was unexpectedly fatal for him. Among the users, there was a feeling of sharing a common fate. He was one of us, one from our group; I was shocked and should have declared drugs to be my archenemy, to hate them and to get them out of my life forever, to radically reject them. Undoubtedly there were people who, after the death of Ferry, were so shocked that they immediately stopped using drugs. However, I, along with many others, didn't. For a while, we were more careful and for a time had the illusion that we had them well in hand, that we wouldn't be so dumb as to overdose or to mix too many different drugs.

In the meantime, drugs showed their true nature to the world. The film *Christian F* was released, and everyone could see the distorted world of drug addiction. It was clear; drugs are no mind expanders, no innocent luxury, but a determined people-killer. Increasingly, at the end of each month, we collected the rent and divided up the loot. Fred and I were using more and more drugs and were beginning to physically deteriorate. In an angry moment,

I broke up with my girlfriend because I suddenly felt trapped. At night, we sometimes broke into places; and when "our tenants" began not paying their rent, we threatened them with violence.

The tension began to greatly increase because some of our tenants turned out to be junkies and, therefore, were in no position to pay. Increasingly, the house became a meeting house for users, with disastrous results for the interior. Fred and I regularly went to Paris to visit a dimly lit club. We took speed with us, which was deadly dangerous because France was fanatic in its drugs policy. Many a Netherlander had to spend many years in French prisons because of it.

Once, there was a fight in the club, which led to the ruin of the beautiful staircase. The building deteriorated, and the situation became impossible. My own situation also deteriorated. To top it all, it appeared that I had picked up a venereal disease from a girl. With the prescription for antibiotics, I went, overexcitedly, to the chemist; and when, for some reason or other, they wouldn't give me the medicine, my frustration came to a boiling point, and in blind anger, I smashed to smithereens the window where you hand in your prescription. The glass flew all around, and with a bloody hand, I went out into the street. Swearing, I came to the first aid station, where my wound was stitched up. Physically and mentally, I felt broken. After the treatment, while a nurse was bringing me to another section of the hospital, I looked furtively left and right. Perhaps I could get hold of some "medication" here.

While I was wandering around the hospital looking for medication and the exit, two cops suddenly came walking toward me.

I quickly looked for an escape route, but the policemen's steps quickened.

At the station, the policemen asked for the facts of the case.

"You can drop dead, write up the charge, and let me go," I yelled. The cops shrugged their shoulders and typed the report. I yearned for a shot. I wanted rest . . .

"You can go and get your medicine now," said the cop. "They made a mistake and thought that you didn't have insurance."

After a half hour, I was outside, standing on the stoop in front of the station.

The street noises sounded like hammer blows in my ears.

I have to get money and go to a dealer. Like a crazy person, I strode through the center of town and, at a certain moment, grabbed some cash out of the drawer of a cash register. All around me was noise; the mass of people made it possible for me to get away, the yearning for dope a cocoon. It had all happened in a second, it seemed, as I deeply inhaled the heroine smoke at the dealer's and held it in as long as possible, so as to profit to the maximum from the effect of the drug. Intoxication and anaesthesia—able to get off the fast train for a little while! Bathed in sweat, with a terrible headache, I came to the next day.

I remembered "the chemist."

As weak as a kitten, I started out again to get my medicine. I noticed the smashed window had been replaced.

"Look, stupid," I said and lifted my bandaged hand to show the lady behind the glass.

Coolly, she gave me antibiotics and looked past me to greet the next customer. Anger welled up in me, and I felt like smashing the window again but managed to control myself.

"Hope you also catch something." Disconsolately, I again went out on to the street. "What could she do about it, the cow."

"I have to get out of this," I decided, and my thoughts went out to distant beaches. "Why should I let myself be rapidly dragged further down the road?"

I was amazed at my own determination and firm intention.

CHAPTER 7

TRAVELING

I quickly made my plans, and that week, I sold everything that I could call my own and counted the result: about one thousand guilders.

Fred, who knew about my plans, discovered where I had hidden the money and took it in an unguarded moment. When I went to get the money, I was shocked to find that it was gone. Only Fred knew about it. When I saw him jauntily coming across the street that afternoon in a brand-new pair of boots, I was certain.

"Dog," I yelled in his face, "pay that money back."

"Yeah, yeah," he hushed me, not denying it. "You shouldn't hide your money in such a stupid place," he said scornfully, knowing that because of his physical power, there wasn't much I could do about it. "Easy now; you'll get it back," he said again, trying to calm me.

It was probably just a quirk, but that week, he had a stroke of good luck financially and gave me my money back. Quickly, I gathered up some things in my sleeping bag and immediately left for Paris.

Eventually, it was to be a trip of four months, looking for kicks in a rotten world. A trip via Paris, Nice, Switzerland, Yugoslavia, Athens, Crete, and Haifa, ending up under the walls of Jerusalem. The first days, my body was afflicted by the physical withdrawal from heroine. It was the first of many times that were to come. I defied my pain and regarded it as a kick, too.

I praised the day that I again felt fit, my reward for keeping at it. "But what now?" I asked myself.

In Nice, I saw that drug use had a real grip on the wandering youth. I heard about all kinds of abusive situations—stealing from each other, living in vacation homes, breaking and entering, etc. I quickly decided to continue traveling. In rich Switzerland for two days, car owners in their marvelous cars arrogantly passed me by, so that I had to continue by train. In Athens, I drank myself silly with ouzo with a guy who had just got out of military service. He told me some facts about how rough the right-wing Greek government treated its citizens who "thought differently." Three years of disciplinary training in compulsory service had broken him. Under the majestic columns of the Acropolis, an unsuccessful hotel manager tried to involve me in sex tourism. There was a whole scene that based its earnings on older but wealthy American women who longed for a man. They met the "need" and figuratively and literally completely undressed the women. I understood from the hotel manager that the art of it was to get them drunk and then, after "servicing" them, to steal their jewelry.

Easy money, but not for me.

I left for Crete where the magnificence of the Mediterranean Sea gave a wonderful refreshing feeling. In Mattela's grotto, a pilgrimage place for hippies in the sixties, I found peaceful simplicity with the friendly population. There you had the lady fruit seller, with a caring smile, add an extra orange to the fruit that was already very cheap. In the rock-ringed bay, campfires were lit in the evening, around which the younger people gathered. Well-known pop tunes played on the guitar mixed in with the sound of the eternal surf.

It was good staying around there, and I finally settled in. I traveled around for a while with a Swede. In colorful language, we told each other exaggerated tales about our travel adventures.

Unbelievable! His stories about Jerusalem and the Dead Sea made me long to go to that country. Through his stories, he interested me in Israel. I already respected that land because of its location among so many powerful enemies.

I could have enjoyed my rest for quite some time if he hadn't started talking about it. When he also told about the possibility to work in a kibbutz, it became clear to me that I must go there and right away. The following day, I bought a ticket with the last of my money. The ticket was for a flight from Crete to Athens and from Athens by boat to Haifa. It was a beautiful sight from the airplane to see the islands, laying like pearls in the clear blue sea. How heavenly beautiful is creation. The boat was full of young traveling people from many countries. After one-and-a-half days, we arrived in the Middle East.

It was bad luck, but I didn't have one cent to my name. While walking around the medieval-looking harbor of Haifa, a man came up to me and pointed to my leather jacket.

"Sell, sell," he called.

I hadn't thought of that. I had a leather jacket that was worth money, and in this climate, I really didn't need it, so I negotiated with the man and ended up with forty pounds.

Stupid of me because I had been reckoning in English pounds. With good humor, I first treated myself to some ice cream. I ordered a large one and was shocked to have to pay eight pounds for it. On questioning, I found out that a pound was worth only a Dutch quarter, but the dealer had disappeared.

I am not really attached to possessions, and I soon forgot about it, despite the fact that with the rest of the money I could just pay for a bus ticket to Tel Aviv. Through the kibbutz office in Tel Aviv I landed up in Kibbutz Shiller in Rehobot. I worked there for a month and met many people and learned how to pick oranges and to take care of avocados. It was good staying there and my respect for Israel grew. Once, when I was with two young ladies from the kibbutz drinking tea on a terrace in an Arab city on the West Bank, some Arabs suddenly began negotiating with me with regard to the ladies. At first, I couldn't believe my ears; the ladies felt very uneasy. We thought that it was high time to return to the kibbutz.

As I wanted to see the country, I left the kibbutz and began to travel around. I read a newspaper floating in the Dead Sea, dove into the coral-rich Red Sea, and plodded for hours through the Sinai.

With a dry, thirsty throat, I looked through my backpack, where I found two warm cans of beer. The liquid quickly went to my head. In the sunny, yellow landscape I discovered a three-feet-long, cream-colored lizard. An aggressive impulse came over me, and with a great deal of pleasure, I ran after the beast. The creature knew its way and quickly disappeared into a crack in the rock at the side of the road. Crazily, I started pulling out some stones until I remembered that there could be scorpions laying under them. Panting, I drunkenly looked around me, while the road quivered, reflecting off the heat.

Fortunately, there were understanding car drivers. At last, I woke up at the Jaffa Gate of Jerusalem, just at the time when a Netherlands tour group came along. Wow, Jerusalem, the contested city. Jerusalem with its religious atmosphere, where so many well-known historical events had taken place. And what did it do to me? It impressed me. But I was an outsider, a tourist, an onlooker—one who couldn't sympathize with the feelings of the religious people. Muslims, Christians, and Jews. What moved them? I visited the Wailing Wall and saw that the Jews were happy with their memorial. There was an atmosphere of hospitality. I felt that I was welcome.

There, where it was forbidden for the women to walk on the holy place, I could approach the massive stones on which the Wailing Wall rested and see the petitions of thousands of Jews written on papers that were stuck into cracks between the stones of the huge wall. So many people, so many wishes. Wishes of shalom.

On the Temple Mountain, I visited the Mosque of Omar. Before going inside, I had to take off my shoes and wash my feet, which I found very appropriate. Here, on top of Mount Zion, Abraham had wanted to sacrifice his son Isaac, but he was held back by God as He himself would provide a sacrifice. I remembered that both Arabs and Jews were descendants of Abraham. From the Temple Mountain, I looked out over the city and saw the many impressive towers.

Whatever people may say, here you must, in any event, come to believe that there is a God. But which God? History lessons teach that the different religions haven't had it easy with each other down through the ages. On the contrary, there were times when people killed each other off. Below, the Jews pray; up here, the Muslims; in the church, Christians. And who listens in Heaven? Why would a murderer be allowed to come into a place so beautiful? Whoever preached murder and death in the name of God would surely not come in, I reasoned. I had, in any event, no contact with Heaven.

When I came down, the exhaust fumes from chugging city buses brought me back to the twentieth century. Above the big bus station, a strangely shaped rock formation could be seen—Golgotha.

Later, I talked about the centuries-old Jewish-Arab conflict and faith with a pleasant, hash-smoking, but extremely hospitable rabbi and heard about how the two people groups, in fact, had the same founding father, Abraham.

The conflict was, therefore, according to my companion, an out-of-control family argument.

On a bus, I met a couple of Israeli girls who invited me to come and visit them. When sometime later I was in the area of the city where they lived, I decided to visit them. The address turned out to be in a busy working-class neighborhood, and I was led there by the boys from whom I asked the way to the address in question. However, I didn't see those girls during the whole week I stayed there because they were in military service. The compulsory service time for girls was two years. The many children took me along to the beach and proudly introduced me to their neighbors as their Dutch guest. At the end of the week, the father called me in to see him. A brother translated with a serious face. Father, with his classical Eastern features, looked at me meaningfully. In a movie, he could have played the part of a wise village elder.

What I understood was that Pa could find work for me. And through the window, he pointed to one of his daughters in the back garden, whom he said I could marry.

She was very pretty—I had already noticed—but this was all beginning to get too serious. When I took leave of this hospitable family, I was given some tomatoes and an egg to take along. Through acquaintances from the kibbutz where I had worked, I met a man who offered me some paid work—ten hours a day, six days a week, Sabbath free.

I worked for over a month at a building company and so was able to buy my airplane ticket back to the Netherlands. For my believing mother, I took a cedar wood statue of Moses from the Holy Land. Just outside Schiphol Airport in Amsterdam, the canals and the lush green of the meadows gave me the feeling that I had stepped back into a completely different world.

Back in The Hague, I decided to stay off the dope. Healthy and tanned from the sun, I felt good; but the very first weekend, it went wrong, and I was sorry that I had come back to the Netherlands.

CHAPTER 8

THE ARMY

My life fell quickly into the same old pattern—working via a job placement agency, going out, and using drugs.

One morning, a neat, brown envelope appeared in my mailbox. I was curious as I picked it up. "Defense" was printed on it. *Oh, oh*, I thought, *that's what it is.*

A long time ago, I had also received an envelope like this. But the call-up for compulsory military service came at an inconvenient time for me, and I had thrown it into the circular file. I tore the letter open and read, "Required physical examination in connection with immediate military service . . . if you don't appear on the mentioned date and time a judicial procedure by the military court may result in imprisonment . . . blah, blah."

Compulsory military service—maybe not such a bad idea, I thought, as I walked back upstairs. Once in my room, I saw the drug equipment laying there. I thought, *Maybe it would be better for me to go into the army for a while; perhaps, it'll smarten me up, and I can get more direction in my life through the discipline I'll learn there. Anyhow, I'll be taken care of, and maybe I can pay some of the traffic fines that are adding up to a tidy sum because of driving without a license . . .* The more I thought about it, the more I began to like the idea. On the given day, I drove my six-cylinder Buick Skylark that I had bought someplace for the ridiculously low price of six hundred guilders and which drove especially well to the military camp in Breda. There, I was put in a group with a number of other daredevil types. I could see that this group of guys had reported only because of the threat of being prosecuted if they didn't. In my time, it was "in" to evade compulsory service for one reason or another.

The most varied lot of advice was passed around with regard to being declared medically unfit. These ranged from pretending to be deaf or color blind, to acting very dumb, to looking crazy, to saying that you had phobias or a mother complex or fear of water or of catching a disease. Another way, it was said, was not to wash for a while and to wear stinking clothes to the medical examination.

"What about getting stoned for a couple of days, so that you look like a corpse?" joked an acquaintance. Many guys succeeded in getting the coveted S5—of unsound mind—or some such thing and boasted about this with great hilarity in the scene. This made a difference of eighteen months in service. Those eighteen months you could spend in a better way, it was thought, and anyone who could get around the medical service by way of a trick had done well in our circles. In any event, Fred was successful in one way or another, so the so-called "brother service" did not apply to me, and that was that.

I had decided that it was better for me to do my military service. As soon as I had presented myself at the base, I had to go to the captain for a personal talk. After chatting about one thing or another and showing my goodwill, I asked if he would do me the favor of assigning me to the driver's training. "If I have a driving license for trucks, I can integrate better into society," was my plea.

The physical lasted two days, and the group of late-comers had to stay overnight in the barracks. The talk in this group was mainly about the best tricks and pretended sicknesses that could serve the result we wanted—namely, to be declared physically unfit. Furthermore, there was the usual macho talk, but for the rest, it went okay. There was a strange guy from Groningen—in the eyes of the people from the West of the country, everyone from Groningen was strange. Now, in the barracks, he remained sitting fully dressed on his bed, while everyone else undressed or washed themselves in preparation for the night. When the last person was finished and wanted to turn out the light and asked him if he didn't want to wash, he mumbled that the light could be turned off. Once this was done, you could tell from the noises he made that he was lying down—with his clothes and boots on, that is.

The following morning, when I woke up, he was sitting beside his bed. Trick or not, it worked, and the guy was called away during breakfast and was nowhere to be seen in the second part of the physical. Maybe the guy from Groningen was not so dumb after all.

The afternoon of the physical, we were told the results. I passed my physical and got a note from the captain with the address of a base in the city of Tilburg. "After the weekend, report at 8:00. It is a driver's training course," he said dryly. "Make something of it." I had to admit that I was really glad. Fortunately, we could immediately claim our travel costs at an office in the camp because my Buick was a gas guzzler! With the money I got, I reckoned I could make it to The Hague. Smart Westerner. To directly cheat a self-service gas station doesn't seem so cool to me now.

During the weekend, I sold the big car for a good price and was able to get hold of an old DAF car in its place. The thing looked awful, but I didn't need to keep fooling around to get gas, and also in the big car, I was more easily picked up for driving without a license.

The following Monday morning, I was on my way, well-motivated, to a new experience. From no licence to a truck driver's license is crazy. I decided to take up the driver training seriously so that I would be finished with all that license garbage once and for all. The excuses I used when I was caught by the police were well known: I forgot to take my license with me. By chance, I had the car ownership papers with me, but I didn't have my license. The police aren't stupid, and they could tell that something was wrong. But, they stuck to the rules—namely, that the next day you had to come to the station and show your driving license. If you didn't, that meant a hefty fine had to be paid. They kept track of how often you were caught, and the more that happened, the higher the fine.

You could, of course, go to jail instead of paying, but you don't do that for the fun of it. And so altogether, I had paid thousands of guilders in fines.

Now I'd finally get my license and be rid of all that misery. Also, I thought that I would learn some self-discipline, but because of something that unexpectedly happened, the plans didn't work out as I had thought.

CHAPTER 9

EEF

Aside from the fact that I had a helmet that was much too big, life in the camp was fine.

It was during the third weekend leave that I was in my favorite night spot in Scheveningen—Hans and Gretel. It was love at first sight with a beautiful doll. This was at the bar, from which you had a good view out to the entrance so that you could always see directly who was coming in. At a certain moment, an acquaintance came in with a girl that I couldn't keep my eyes off! Of course, there are a lot of pretty girls in such places, and I had had several girlfriends; but this time, something happened to me that had never happened before.

I felt so strongly attracted to her. I didn't only see two huge, blue eyes in a peaches-and-cream complexion and beautiful, long, wavy, gold-colored hair but also a magical smile. I hopped off my bar stool and went over to introduce myself to her. I don't remember what I said, but I had the impression that she enjoyed meeting new people. My acquaintance was not too pleased with my pushiness in introducing myself to this girl, and I could appreciate his displeasure!

Back with my friend at the bar, I naturally didn't want to let him see that I really went for this girl. I made a joke, saying that certainty was important in life—and it was certain that gold-colored beer should always be fresh and gold-colored tapped—but a woman, regardless of how gold-colored she was, would always eventually become gray.

"Still, many will choose the last rather than the first, and so there will be more in the barrel," he countered.

"Maybe we should give a lot of thought to both," we decided laughingly. We decided we were going to play up to her, and he was going to be the first to try. Now, he was not the bravest guy, and he was a bit awkward on this subject, even though he was quite good-looking. With some insistence, we finally got her address from my acquaintance.

The very next day, we planned that my friend should stop by her house and invite her to go out with the two of us that evening. She still lived with her parents, and they weren't at home.

The following day, I watched from a short distance away as he rang her doorbell. The door opened; they talked; and he went inside.

This is going okay, I thought, *unless it's going too good.*

After I had been impatiently waiting for some time, the door opened, and my friend appeared. When he came up to me, I thought he looked rather pale.

"And?" I asked inquisitively.

"My visit was not appreciated," he answered.

"What do you mean?" I prodded him.

"She didn't have her makeup on," he said sarcastically.

"Really?" I asked.

"Really," he replied.

"And tonight?" I asked with a weak smile because I had a feeling that he had messed it up.

"She'll go," he replied with little enthusiasm.

"Now, great," I shouted.

As we walked along, I got the rest of what had happened out of him. It seemed that during the visit, while I was waiting outside, not much was said because they both were feeling shy, and as I already said, he didn't do so great in this kind of situation. She flipped because she didn't have her makeup on, and he couldn't handle that with a joke of some kind. There were painful silences, and then he had had enough. If he once let such an emotional barrier develop, then he couldn't easily handle it.

These developments were to my advantage, I reckoned, and my friend decided not to join us that evening, and so we began to go out. She didn't have a particular boyfriend, but I had seen that I wasn't the only one she went around with. I was in love with her, but she wasn't in love with me. My continual advances and the effort I made to get her attention and the trouble I had convincing her that I was a special guy, even though I drove a DAF car, succeeded, much to my great satisfaction, needless to say. The others weren't worthy of her, I decided.

All these unexpected developments meant that it was only late Monday morning that I recovered from the weekend. Oh, yeah, the camp—first, report in sick. Oh, I regretted it that just now, when this brilliant thing was happening to me, I was in the army and had to waste the whole week on the base and fight against the urge to get out of there.

The next weekend, after a week that seemed like forever, I raced as fast as my DAF would go to my girlfriend. If only I still had the eight-cylinder, I could be in The Hague twice as fast. But I also thought maybe I would run out of gas halfway, so I was happy with this coffee grinder with which, with one tank of gas, you could drive to Paris. And maybe I'll do that with her, too, I fantasized during the trip.

When I arrived in The Hague, it appeared that her parents had gone to visit family in Australia. They would be away for a couple of months! This gave rise to new possibilities, and I quickly went to live at her house.

The following Monday morning, after a heavy weekend, I was too spaced out to think about the base. I couldn't get away, and I didn't want to.

Eef asked me, "Can't that cause you problems?"

We had to laugh at that. We couldn't care less, so we had a great time and didn't hear anything from the base for a month. What luxury to be able to use a whole house. This was living—everything I needed was right there. I got dressed and went into the living room to see if Eef had made something that could be called breakfast. There was a strong, sweet smell, and when I came into the living room, there was a thick cloud of marijuana smoke. Eef sat on a chair fiddling with her pipe.

She looked up and smiled. "Is there anything to eat?" I asked as I opened the door into the garden.

"Maybe in the kitchen; look there and get something for me, too, please," she said with a sweet look on her face.

I thought she was pretty. "Okay, but have you been smoking for a long time?" I asked.

"I began in school so as to be one of the gang, but now I like it," she replied.

"But you get really spaced out from that stuff. I've tried it, and I had the feeling that for hours a jet plane was flying around in my head. What a lot of garbage that is," I said.

"Well, I like having flies and butterflies going through my head," she answered. Fortunately, the smoke went out the door to the garden. I went to the kitchen and brought back bread, jam, and butter to the living room. "Did you finish school?" I asked.

"I had a nice job, but I couldn't concentrate. And you know what I hated?" she asked.

"No," I replied.

"Well, I was always good in math. I understood it easily until I smoked for a week, and then I couldn't understand it anymore. So, at a certain point, I quit school and went to work."

"That's what you get," I teased her.

"But my work is okay," she continued.

"Mine, too," I answered, while I held up my ID tag that hung around my neck. "The dog tag," I joked.

"And I'm curious to know when they're coming to let you out." She laughed.

And sometime that week, the doorbell rang, and I knew instinctively that they had come for me. I shot out the kitchen door into the garden and snuck over the fence. Eef received the police and let them look through the house.

Of course, they knew that I was somewhere but stopped searching. From then on, I knew it wouldn't be long before I was in their hands and that the party would be over. A couple of days later, I went out on an errand and suddenly found myself surrounded by blue jackets. For days, I was kept in a cell. Finally, I was taken to the military prison in Nieuwersluis.

NIEUWERSLUIS

Real punishment was not in Nieuwersluis. Every day, we had sports and a lot of time for relaxation outside our cells. My fellow prisoners were in for various infringements of the law. In the main, it was for drunk driving. This was also the infringement for which most of the officers were in detention. Of course, the officers sat in a separate area and had their sports programs and other activities apart from the "normal" soldiers. Without doubt, they had it a bit better. In my section were various people in for alcohol abuse and desertion, but only a few for use of force. One had beat up a captain during drill. That man had gotten a heavy punishment. There was also a special case in our wing, namely a conscientious objector. He had the strictest regime possible in the detention center.

Cell punishment. That meant for eighteen months, you spent the whole day in your cell, no contact with other detainees, and no sport or other activities outside the cell. Airing at set times. On the one hand, I respected people who were willing to accept the consequences of their actions. On the other hand, I couldn't approve this refusal to go into the Dutch army, which was clearly a defense-oriented army and necessary to protect the democracy we had obtained against dictatorial systems. Freedom of speech, press, assembly, and religion were matters worth defending, I thought. I had to think back to the time of the Nazis. Against such a power it is certainly permissible to defend yourself tooth and nail. Those who refused to serve in the Nazi army were brave.

In the context of my own life, it was difficult to make moral judgments. The objector got piles of mail each day from other pacifists, most likely. In any event, he got strong encouragement in his fight, and he knew that he had support and maybe felt happy. Although I can't really believe that.

The only love letters that I have ever written in my life were written here, and it helped because Eef came with her brother-in-law to visit. In the cell next to me sat someone who had already been there for seven months, and he had a long time yet to go. He told me that he would again like to spend a weekend with his girlfriend. That I could understand, and I felt for him. Once a week, on Wednesday, there was a mandatory march of about ten miles around Nieuwersluis. This march was not popular among the men. All prisoners had to take part in it, except those who were sick. So each Wednesday morning, there was a noticeable number of sick reports during roll call after the flag was raised. A person reporting sick didn't need to take part if he had been to the doctor. Only the doctor could declare that the sick report was justified. Moreover, the rumor was that the doctor was homosexual, so if you said a few loving words to him, you had a really good chance of not having to go on the march. Anyway, one morning, there was, noticeably, not one sick report. My neighbor had made known that on the day of the March he was going to try to escape so that he could spend the weekend with his girlfriend. We were all in a good mood and high spirits when we started out that morning.

It was a cold winter, and the lakes around Nieuwersluis were frozen, although the ice was declared unsafe. If, during the march, you had to take a pee—and that happened frequently—then you had to give the duty sergeant a sign. The sergeant then let the group halt. You could pee against a tree and then quickly return to your place in the group so that the march could continue. Also that morning, we had to stop regularly for urinating. When, at a given moment, we were marching over a dike between two lakes, my neighbor reported that he had to go.

The group halted at the command of the sergeant. Gerrit stepped onto the ice to pee. Gerrit didn't turn around but kept on walking further over the ice.

"Hey, are you afraid we'll see you? You've gone far enough," yelled the duty sergeant.

But Gerrit didn't look up and just kept walking. The hilarity now really broke out.

"Greetings to your old woman," we laughingly yelled at him.

"Shut up," said the sergeant, as he finally understood what was going on. "Come back immediately," he ordered.

But Gerrit was determined and pretended he didn't hear. The sergeants didn't go on to the ice themselves because the unsafe signal had been given and also because there would then be too few sergeants remaining with the group. The chance was that there would be more attempts to escape or even that the whole group would run off because at such a moment the spirit of mischievousness could easily turn into rebellion.

The temptation to collectively run away was great at that point. The "why not?" feeling went through the group like a gust of wind, but something held them back. For me, at any rate, it would have been foolish to try to escape considering that I was in detention for only a month.

The military police were called out to comb the whole neighborhood while we stood watching in the cold. Now we had a great time because our pal wasn't caught, but in the meantime, we longed for a cup of hot chocolate. In order to get their own back, they let us stand, teeth chattering, for a few hours in the snow.

The following Monday, Gerrit appeared at the gate to report. We saw him being taken away with his thumb up for our benefit. He got three weeks isolation, but he had had his weekend.

After my detention, I was again in regular service. Now I was placed somewhere else—in the canteen service. I had blown my chance to get a driver's license, and so now I could sweep out tents. I was in a good group, and we had a great time. We had to go to Germany for an exercise. There was a guy in our unit that was of no use. He wanted out from the service, and he simulated a so-called mother complex. If his mother was not around—and in the army, that is usually the case—then his social and practical functioning was paralyzed.

In Germany, our unit experienced its first big exercise. We had to carry out an exercise and set up all the tents and storehouses. And just as we had finally finished in the middle of the night, a captain rode onto the field and announced that we were in the wrong place. That meant taking everything down and rebuilding it all again, a hundred yards further up. The announcement certainly did not improve the atmosphere in the group. We were all freezing cold, and there was a thick layer of snow on the ground.

Even in these difficult conditions, Koos clung to his simulation of a mother complex. Which meant that he didn't put a finger out to help. Now, he was really an object of our scorn. Everything that wasn't nailed down was thrown at him. After many hours of work, we were finally finished with the new camp. The last thing we did was to warm up our tent with gas stoves and roll our sleeping bags out. Finally, we could all go to sleep, and the last person turned out the light.

The very last one was Koos, who came in after the light had already been turned off. He crawled into bed but didn't suspect that we had decided that anyone who didn't help put up the tents also couldn't sleep in one. So, the minute he slipped into his sleeping bag, some of the guys picked him up and put him—sleeping bag and all—outside the tent in the snow. A loud laugh arose from our tent.

"I'll throw him in the lake," yelled someone. Koos would have been a block of ice in a second.

The exercise lasted for two weeks, and we had to take care of provisions. At the end of the two weeks, back at the camp, our work involved cleaning and repairing equipment that had been used during the exercise, an awful job. The malingering of Koos was not rewarded by permission to get out of service early, despite all the sacrifices he made. In the meantime, I realized that the rest of my military service would consist of a repeat of three times the type of exercise we had just been through.

In connection with the economic retrenchment, we were allowed only one shooting exercise where everyone got the chance to shoot a maximum of twenty bullets. Because my helmet was too big and kept falling over my eyes when I shot, I always missed the target. Once, we got a hand grenade, which we had to throw into the dunes.

"And don't throw away the pin instead of the grenade" was said three times. I was relieved to see that I was not in the group with Koos. You never know with such a jerk.

Once, according to a rumor around the platoon, a soldier had accidentally dropped a hand grenade in the middle of the platoon. The regular army duty sergeant had fallen on the grenade and thereby offered his own life to save the lives of the men.

The following exercise was coming up. In the meantime, I was on drugs, especially in the weekends. Someone told me that using drugs in service was punishable by immediate dismissal. The same week I went to the doctor to tell him that I was using, whereby he sent me immediately to Utrecht to see a psychiatrist. When I got there, the only thing the psychiatrist asked me was if I wanted to stay in service. I answered honestly that I had no desire to stay. That was enough because he signed a paper that freed me from any further responsibilities with regard to military service.

Within a day, to my great surprise, I was again a normal citizen. When I went to get my clothes from the barracks I met up with my old comrades, who were just as surprised as I was that I only had to report once, and I was finished and could go home. When I saw Koos at the barracks, I could give him this golden tip, but it didn't help him.

When I stood outside the barracks gate, I tore up my military passport and threw it in the trash can that hung on a pole by the bus stop. I kept only the page with my photo to save for my children.

An advantage of military service was that I had gotten my drug use somewhat under control. In the free weekends, I had used some, but it didn't take over my life. Physically, I was in good condition. I decided again to cut back on drugs. But the next weekend, I didn't succeed in being drug-free.

Back in The Hague, I rented an attic flat, and Eef came to stay with me on weekends. In the meantime, my drug use began to take on a grim form. One day during the week, the sister of Eef appeared at the door. Strange time for a visit.

"What's the matter?" was my immediate question.

"Eef is in the hospital; she's having trouble with her heart."

She had got an infection in her heart valve because of using drugs.

Now she can stop, I thought, because to my mind she used much too much. Maybe it was good that she was there. However, all the activity connected with my getting drugs meant that I didn't go to visit her.

CHAPTER 10

SPAIN

That week, Bernard, an old friend, came around.

"Hey, Rem, how's it going?" he came in, cheerful as usual, and handed me a piece of spekkoek, a type of Indonesian layer cake.

"Fine. Good to see ya, Bernard. Are you still working in the same spekkoek shop?"

"Yeah, I have to do something with all my time. Incidentally, do you have anything in the house?" he asked.

"You know that I can't keep it, mate; if I have it, it's used immediately," I answered. "Cup of tea?"

"Yeah, give me that then."

"Have you got a smoke?" I asked him from the kitchen.

"Shag," and he gave it to me.

"And what else?" I asked.

"I've been wanting for years to finish my studies," he replied, "but you know how it is—with dope, no hope. Rem, I want to get clean, and that's why I'm here. Because I know that you're always busy trying to stop. Can't we do it together?"

"Going clean, I'm all for that, but as you know, it's always using to stop using and seeing how you get back on it," I responded dryly. "Do you know what I find the best fun?"

"No," answered Bernard.

"When I see you standing there, shivering!"

"Thanks."

"Now that winter is coming, it's not such a good idea, but I want to go abroad and just stay away for a while," Bernard told me.

I began to find abroad more interesting now. *If I get off drugs abroad and Eef stops in the hospital, maybe we could make a new beginning,* I thought to myself. We drank tea and fantasized freely.

I suddenly remembered that my mother had once told me about a Christian movement in Spain.

"Call her up," suggested Bernard.

The idea excited us. After several telephone calls, I got hold of the address.

"It's the hard-as-rock method, you understand, don't you? Are you sure you want to do it?" my acquaintance persisted.

We decided that we would just hitchhike out of the country. The distance between us and the dealers would become greater, and we would be sick as dogs. But the time it would take to come back would be the same as if we kept going, so we decided we would head south, where it's warm.

The next day, we stood with some of our things and with the money that we had managed to scrape together alongside the highway trying to get a lift. The second day, we felt like snails that had salt thrown over them, but we kept going. After Paris, we couldn't get a lift together, so we agreed that we would each hitch alone and meet each other at our destination.

After some days, during which I had pulled myself through feeling like a drunken dog, I finally arrived. It was a tourist-like Baptist conference center. The verger heartily received me, despite the fact that I just turned up out of the blue and he didn't know me. I could stay there for free as long as I wanted to. It was near Christmastime. I didn't think that my friend, Bernard, would turn up, and I wondered what had happened to him. In the meantime, I was feeling much better. That weekend, on New Year's Eve, I was invited by someone to go out.

"Okay, why not?"

We left in the afternoon, when it was warm, and had a good time in clubs until late at night. During the day, it was warm, so I was dressed just in shirtsleeves when I started out.

Late at night, the club closed, and everyone went home. Also, the guys who had invited me stepped into a car and suddenly disappeared. There I was, standing alone in the cold of night, while behind me the last neon lights of the club went out. In the dark, I had difficulty orienting myself, and I wondered which way to go. I was getting very cold, so I quickly chose which direction I should take.

After some time, shivering from the cold, I couldn't find the conference center anywhere. In the end, my whole body shook. In a panic, I rang the doorbell of a house. After ringing and waiting for some time, a shutter opened, and a lot of non-understandable Spanish came down accompanied by strong gestures. After all this, the woman slammed the shutter closed without waiting for a response from me. I was dying from the cold. *It would really be ironic to expire from the cold in warm Spain while running away from cold Netherlands because of drugs*, I thought. In the meantime, my muscles started to stiffen from the cold, and I began to panic. Above me, millions of stars blinked down at me from the clear sky.

Then I couldn't go on, and spontaneously, I began to pray, "God, if You help, help me now, please! Please!" In a panic I began to run, and not more than two seconds later, I was suddenly in front of the conference center. Surprised, happy, and grateful, I hurried in to get warm by the stove. The following day, when I went to check out the route, I discovered that the evening before in the cold, I had obviously walked a couple of times past the conference center without realizing it. Interesting that my eyes had suddenly been opened once I had prayed.

Life is confusing, I thought. Where was Bernard? In the meantime, I had been in Spain more than a week, and I decided to return to the Netherlands. By telephone, I had persuaded my mother to send me money for the train.

After two days on the train, I arrived in the Netherlands, starving from hunger. Once in The Hague, I immediately went to look for Bernard. I should not have done that because I found him while he was smoking heroine.

"Where were you, junkie?" I asked him suspiciously.

"I was caught in the tunnel by Lyon—what a crazy situation, man!" he answered, stoned. In a very roundabout way, he told me how his trip had gone wrong.

Near Lyon, he had walked into a tunnel, thinking that he could get a lift on the other side. What he didn't know, though, was that the tunnel was more than two miles long. As he went on, he kept hoping that after the next bend, he would see the light at the end; but unfortunately, after each bend, came yet another bend and, therefore, not the longed for exit. Halfway through, he was suffocating from the exhaust fumes. He was just able to reach an alarm telephone, but he didn't know how it worked. In panic, he began to stop cars going through the tunnel, which led to a total traffic jam. Because he had taken the phone off the hook, the police were alarmed. Also, the fire truck had been called out—in truth, it was one big mess! An automobilist had finally brought him out of the tunnel. There, he finally caught his breath and was held for several hours for questioning by the gendarmerie.

Because of the scare, he wasn't able to go on further and returned directly to The Hague. A sniff of heroine to recover from the fright was his excuse for using again.

"Stupid," I accused him, "now we've done everything for nothing."

"But not you," he said.

"Yes, but we were going to do it together—together be addicted, together get clean—so now give me the rest of the dope," I threatened. I smoked the rest of his heroine. All the hardships were for nothing.

When I finally visited Eef, she was very angry. "Where were you? You didn't really go on vacation while I was in the hospital."

"I went to get clean," I defended my actions. "But it didn't work." She couldn't be calmed down until I played my last trump card—namely, a bottle of wine. One from the supermarket on the corner, but it worked, she changed her tune. Somewhere in the quiet house, we drank up the bottle; and while doing so, things were good between us again.

LIVING TOGETHER

I could rent the floor beneath me, and so I exchanged my attic floor for a somewhat bigger space. When she was allowed to leave the hospital, Eef came to live with me. She had a job at the Central Bureau for Statistics, and together, we could easily make it financially. Shortly afterwards, I applied for a job at the Bijenkorf department store, purely because the window decoration work mentioned in an advertisement appealed to me. Living together suited me. The ice cream shop was only thirty yards away. Further, there was everything that was needed just around the corner—from the milkman to a cafe.

To my great surprise, I was taken on by the Bijenkorf department store as an apprentice window dresser. I had embroidered upon my artistic abilities in the job interview. This, or perhaps the sympathy of the head of the personnel department, had resulted in me being chosen out of more than forty applicants. I was very proud of this and thought it was a nice job. It soon appeared that I had some talent, and the head of personnel had realized this better than I myself had. I could make up windows and displays. Also, I could help with setting up the gallery for the exhibition of works of various artists. My work was satisfactory, but my social skills were not well-developed. I had trouble with finding something in common with my colleagues. My long weekends meant that I wasn't always fit, to put it mildly. I could hardly make it in the mornings anymore. During lunch hour, I quickly went to a dealer or to the foundation on the Prinsegracht and smoked myself "fit" with heroine, so that the day's earnings were thus used up.

The foundation subsidized by the city was a kind of assistance place for addicts. Downstairs, there was social space, and upstairs, for five guilders, you could get a reasonable meal. Most of the visitors were between the ages of eighteen and thirty. In my opinion, the foundation helped people go further down into the pit rather than to get out of it. In the toilet, there was a long wash basin with four faucets next to each other, like you see in barracks and shelters. Everyone was there setting up a shot or taking one. Sometimes, the wash basin was covered with blood from shots that didn't work.

Those who often took a shot were sometimes busy for a quarter of an hour trying to get the needle somewhere into a vein because the walls of the veins were hardened with calluses, right up to the neck. Sometimes, there was vomit in and around the wash basin and on the floor because the heroin that was injected irritated the stomach and the junkie heaved everything out right after putting it in. Others stayed hours in the toilet, stoned. Now and then, junkies stole heroine from one another just before it was to be used, and an argument or a fight broke out. A couple of times, an addict lost consciousness, and there was a commotion. There was a great amount of dealing in all kinds of drugs and also in stolen goods. Junkies came there together as at a kind of base for going out on raids in the center of The Hague.

In the "foundation," you came up against everything—from long-term junkies to Germans who had come over and were really ripped off when buying dope, to school kids who wanted to act "heavy" and boys from a trailer camp who came to steal from the dealers. It was there that I first met Rinus. He was older than I, and when he was there, he smoked along. For one reason or another I liked him, and we always got together for a chat. Typical for this guy was that sometimes you didn't see him in the foundation but in the Weversplaats in the city. He stood there singing, along with a group of half-hippies. Led by a guitar, the guys sang about stars in the Heaven, certainly not my kind of music!

As I later understood, this group were "Jesus people." A couple of weeks after I had seen him singing so sweetly in the city, I met him in the foundation playing the smoker's tube, stoned.

"You belong to the Jesus group on the other side of the Prinsegracht," I said to him, very surprised. He mumbled something and indifferently waved away the subject of our talk.

"A bit contradictory, isn't it, to proclaim the faith and then use drugs—or does anything go? Why believe then, if you can't get the strength to get off dope?" I challenged him. With his typical smile, he charmed everyone, and no one could be angry with him for long; but still, I couldn't understand much about the double life he led.

After I was "refreshed" in my lunch hour, I quickly went back to the Bijenkorf and tried to finish my day's work in an afternoon. This was the period when every now and then, dealers would create so-called "crises." Then, a little at a time, heroine was put on the market in order to hike up the price, and the prices could go up three to four times. Sometimes, there was nothing available. If you went into the foundation then, everyone sat there shaking and feeling sick.

That collective mandatory withdrawal somehow made you laugh—certainly, when you saw someone you knew come in with goosebumps and red-rimmed eyes. Some people were aggressive; if a dealer came in, he would be robbed with violence. In order to make optimum use of the scarce heroine, many junkies in a time of crisis switched over from smoking to shooting up with a needle. I was one of them. The physical dependence quickly became stronger. The changeover to injecting was a step further down, a barrier that you didn't break for the fun of it. As a smoker, you always said that you'd never be so dumb as to shoot.

I tried to keep my new method secret from Eef. There were people we knew who began shooting, and because I wanted to protect Eef, I forbade her to begin with this. With the increase in drug use, the tension in our relationship grew. At a certain point, there was regularly something to argue about. The need for drugs grew parallel to the increasing need for money. Our giro balance was long in the red, and for some time, Eef had been getting sickness benefit.

CHAPTER 11
OVERDOSE

The heroine in The Hague was expensive. "In Amsterdam, the dope is cheaper," an acquaintance informed me.

"On the Zeedijk?" I asked him. *If I take more money with me, I can sell it for a profit,* I thought and intended to deal in order to provide for my own use. And indeed, I came back to The Hague with a great deal more dope than I needed. While Eef was busy in the kitchen, I made a strong shot ready for myself.

"Hey, don't take so much at one time," Eef said when she came into the room for a minute. I was already under the influence from smoking, didn't see any difference from other times, and thought that she complained too much.

After a bit of fussing around, the needle was in my vein and a warm glow flowed through my head; then it was dark, and I passed out. I don't know how much time passed until I came to. Amazingly enough, I can still remember the experience very well. It seemed as if I were in a timeless, dark, airless space. I had no visible body; it was neither cold nor warm; there was nothing except my consciousness, and I could see it. Very far above me, I could see vague flickers of light, just as deep-sea divers can see the surface of the ocean mirrored high above. I couldn't move—and that didn't matter—but I felt as though I was rising in an ever-increasing tempo. I kept my eyes fixed upward, focused on the flickering light, which came very close. At a certain moment, an unidentifiable feeling made me intuitively know that I was back in my body. My mouth was the first part of my body that I felt and could localize.

I felt another mouth on mine; it moved in a way that I found pleasant, like the kiss of a woman. Soon after, the feeling returned to the rest of my body, and I could open my eyes. I looked into the tear-stained eyes of Eef, who had given me mouth to mouth resuscitation.

Minutes after this incident, I still had not realized fully what had actually happened. Later, I became well aware that I had almost died and that Eef, in fact, was the instrument that had brought me back. A week later, a couple of acquaintances came to the door—as it goes with junkies—to look each other up, sometimes at the strangest times, to see if there was "something to arrange." That "something" was preferably dope, of course, but money and goods were also okay. You could sometimes "help" someone if he couldn't get rid of stolen goods or if the other person didn't know of a good dealer and you did. Every service was rewarded.

Sometimes the "service" was just company. The need for companionship was strong. If you were broke, you visited acquaintances to see what they had or to arrange something together. I was completely broke, and I wanted a fix. Since I had begun injecting heroine, my longing for drugs had increased. This was in the time when many addicts discovered that several narcotic or stimulant pills could be acquired by means of a prescription from the doctor—pills, strong pain killers, sleeping pills, etc.

Three men strong, we went around the city, stealing in order to get enough money together to get a fix. Often, it was saleable goods that we stole from stores and sold to fences and prostitutes. Some junkies even got lists of goods from "honest" citizens. Cheap though, everything for a third of the price. And the junkies got blamed for it all. Oh, as an addicted person, you very soon learn how people will act just to get a cheap price. If you're an addict, it seems that you're in a circle where everyone is "bad." Of course, junkies can't be tolerated, and the prisons are two-thirds full of them. But that often comes about because we are so obvious and, therefore, more quickly picked up. Others just act less obvious. But good you can't ignore, and we are all responsible for our own deeds.

I don't know now how it all happened, but at a given time, we were in Zoetermeer; and while we were walking through the streets, talking loudly, one of the gang pulled out a box of pills.

"Ya know," he said, "these are things that give you a kick; you really go out of your head!" He put a couple in his mouth and gave me some. "Laugh," he said, acting like a comedian. The other guy also took a couple of pills, with a funny gesture, and I followed his example. Just like naughty schoolboys having great fun imitating each other and doing things that you wouldn't normally do.

Soon afterward, in the train back to The Hague, I felt dizzy. On the way home in the city, I experienced a clear change of consciousness. A sort of drunken feeling, my notion of time disappeared, and I lost much control over my muscles. By the time I got home, I had a good hangover. On the way, I had bought heroine, and the desire for a shot was as great as that of someone in the desert for water. My brother and Eef were at home, and vaguely in the background, I saw them gesturing. Later, they told me that they had tried to convince me not to take a shot. Because of the pills, I had no feeling for the size of the dose nor any control over my muscles and the spoon. Nevertheless, I prepared the shot and put the needle into a vein in my arm. It didn't work, and after several tries, the blood dripped down along my hands.

"Why doesn't that thing go in?" I asked angrily and pushed the needle in deeper—I got it right. The drug went through me, and I sank softly into the dark night.

When I came to, I was all wet, and I saw Eef standing in the room looking very nervous. Still confused and with a swollen tongue, I asked her why she was looking at me like that. Later, Eef told me that I had again passed out and that Fred, who was visiting, had poured water over me. I had had a fit of anger during the blackout and had hit Eef while she was trying to help me.

I remembered nothing and couldn't believe what she said.

BREAKUP

Lia, an old friend of Eef's, came to live on the floor above us. In the meantime, through living on the street, she had become hard and heavily addicted. She always had a lot of money and, thus, drugs, which she let us—and particularly Eef—enjoy with her. I loved Eef very much and wanted the best for her, and she felt the same about me; but because of circumstances, tension and lack of trust were growing between us. Eef sometimes went out with her friend and came home with money. At a certain time, she found out that I was injecting.

She was jealous and angry with me because injecting would give a much greater kick. Without my knowing, she had also begun to inject. I ran into her one afternoon in the "injection" hall of the foundation on the Prinsegracht. Another guy was fiddling around trying to get the needle in her arm. I was furious and couldn't keep myself from giving the junkie a punch and dragging Eef outside. Eef protested, but in a blind rage, I slapped her all the way home, which was a couple of streets away.

Maybe it was the anger that resulted from a feeling of powerlessness and the realization that our relationship would end if it continued in this way. A flashing warning light suddenly rose in me, and, in a panic, I had reacted with violence toward Eef. A distorted cry for help, a call to turn away from the abyss. A cruel way to try to keep someone from injecting. Moreover, I regarded Eef as weaker and one who would go to pieces if I didn't keep her from injecting.

When we got home, the fear came over me that she would leave me, which I would find terrible. My mother talked now and then about prayer, and I forced Eef to pray to God with me. Eef thought that I had gone completely crazy and decided deep in her heart to take the first opportunity she could to get out. For me, an emotional valve had opened, whose existence I had not known about.

"How could I have let myself act like that?" I accused myself later. I understood that I couldn't hold Eef back and also not myself. That week, I fixed Eef her first injection because she couldn't do it herself. Eef was very secure with sterilon against infections.

How the devil would have enjoyed that. Two lovers, Adam and Eve, who helped destroy one another by catching them in their own snare. But we didn't see this invisible world and didn't realize that still greater danger threatened us.

I did my best at work; but I began to come in late, and I often called in sick on Monday mornings. Sometime after these incidents, I came home one evening and, to my great shock, saw that everything belonging to Eef was gone. That was plain to see because all the plants, which were a hobby of hers, had disappeared. The whole place was bare and empty, and I strongly felt the same way. She had really gone. It was over, finished, done with. I felt as though I had lost something very valuable and had the gnawing suspicion that this would be definite. I couldn't control my emotions, and I cried like a little child because of my misery and anger.

That week, I tried to find Eef via her family, but I was told that I had better stay out of her way. At her request, Eef's father had taken her and all her things away; and in their eyes, I was, of course, the big wrong-doer. Not surprisingly, my mother would probably have put all the blame on Eef; that's the way parents often are. It's the same with friends. "He began going around with the wrong people, and then everything went wrong." For parents, the others are always the wrong friends.

After Eef had been gone for some time, I began to think about going to Israel for a couple of years in order to get away from the drug scene. I hadn't been to work for some time and had called in sick. Somehow, I thought that was unfair to my employer, who had given me a real chance, and I decided then to quit. Somehow, I had talent for this kind of work and thought to myself that I'd had some good results with the window displays, the inside lay-out, and setting up of displays. Too bad that I had never heard anything about this until I had a last interview in connection with my resignation.

"We found your work quite good. I'm sorry that it has to end this way," he remarked.

And I thought it was a shame that this had been said only now and not earlier; it might have given me an incentive to carry on and not quit the job so easily. On the other hand, I recognized that drugs would have eventually cost me my job. My plan to go to Israel began to take shape. Somehow, it pepped me up, and at a certain time, I was all wrapped up in it. I'd had a good time is Israel; I could again work in a kibbutz or at the construction company where I had worked for a month. I continued to make my plans.

Meanwhile, because of the cost of my drug habit, I could no longer pay my rent. I stole from stores and made new friends among users. Some of them also injected speed, and I began to do it, too. The speed made us terribly active, and we hardly slept any more. Thoughts about everything kept running through my head. In order to stop that, we used heroine. So it went on for several weeks. We hardly ate anymore, and at a certain time, I was completely depressed and went right off the rails.

I decided to leave everything behind, put some clothes together, and go to Israel. I didn't have a cent, but that was just the stimulus to go away. I owed the landlord money, but people like that were just exploiters in my eyes and could stuff it. With my few possessions, I was ready to go, precisely on the day that I got a check through the mail from the health insurance. I was completely surprised because I had quit my job and had not registered for a benefit. Moreover, I had never before had a payment, so I wasn't used to that convenience. The check was for more than a thousand guilders.

Good pocket money for the journey—getting clean! First, get some new clothes in town, a drink in the Bulldog, and an evening in Scheveningen, I swiftly planned. No sooner said than done, as far as Israel was concerned that was at the end. From dope, yes. That weekend, I spent everything that I had, and it took a couple of days for me to recover.

ROBBERY

Sometime during the week when I was very sick, I had to have drugs. I quickly went to Fred who, according to me, felt as sick as I did. But because many people came to visit him, there was always more of a chance to make arrangements. When he opened the door and I saw him, I knew that he didn't have anything in the house.

Our common thought that was it was better to try to get something with the two of us than alone. That day, the robbery of a gasoline station went amiss. Our only loot was two thick envelopes with accounts and receipts. A misser.

"Now I understand why we weren't followed," said Fred as he threw the pile of papers on the sidewalk.

"I should have tried to grab what was in the cash register," I said.

"Come on, let's knock off a dealer; then we're finished," said Fred, grinning. These vultures were a good target for our aggression. We were ready to cut one's throat. Quickly, we went home to get a knife. I found a suitable bread knife in the kitchen drawer. Together, we drove to the Parallelweg in The Hague, then rode back and forth past a spot where many street dealers were. I sat in the back seat and nodded to a dealer through the window. Then Fred stopped beside a dealer.

"Have you got any heroine for us?" I asked while opening the back door for him.

The jerk stepped in, and Fred stepped on the gas. "Give me four packages," I said, while pretending to take my wallet out of my inside pocket.

I then quickly shoved him aggressively to one side and put the knife to his temple while going through his pockets to see if he might have weapons and other drugs. The dealer let out a couple of shrieks, and after we had taken his stuff, we pushed him out of the car door. We quickly parked the car a couple of streets farther up and finally could smoke. While we were inhaling deeply, we began to feel better and became calmer. A temporary calm, however, that we used to watch Fred's TV completely stoned.

"Did you hear that Coen died?" asked Fred suddenly.

"Coen—who is that?" I gave him a surprised look.

"Oh, you don't know him; he was going somewhere with someone when his friend got out of the car to get a pack of cigarettes, and when he came back, Coen was slumped over in his seat. First, he thought that he was just stoned, but then realized that he was dead. It scared the guy with him to death."

"I can imagine." I nodded. "What if it had happened to you?"

"I think it's that Turkish heroine," Fred continued. "Everyone makes a mistake with that stuff. I tell everyone to take less and be careful, but yeah, they are all as know-it-all as nits. And then you get these kinds of situations. The Chinese are really driven out of the market by the Turks; with their strong heroine, the Turks are hard as rocks. Did you read about the Chinese they found dead in the Amsterdam canals?"

"Clearly war," I responded.

"How much money is involved, do you think?" Fred looked at me.

"Yeah, they just shoot each other, and Coen is no more," I said, all the while asking myself where he was now.

"No, he didn't need a cigarette, old Coen," remarked Fred sarcastically.

I looked at his face to see if he was joking, but he wasn't.

"A while ago, there was also someone who used to come here and now, he's gone, too," said Fred, looking straight at me.

Curious, I looked back at him. "He fell down on the ground, right here in front of me, and stopped breathing. I thought and quickly got some water and threw it over him and revived him, fortunately." Fred was now somewhat agitated.

"I said to the guy after he came to, 'Ya know what you should do?' 'Yeah,' he said. So I said, 'You should stop with that junk, stupid.'" Fred looked at me almost angrily.

"Were you mad at him?" I quickly asked.

"Of course, why should I have this misery in my house? But I was really more fed up with myself; I'm also ruining my life."

In the meantime, I stood up because I couldn't look at him any longer and lit a cigarette while walking to the window to take a look outside.

"We ruin each other in this world, it seems," I said, looking at the monotonous but so well-known facades of the Schilderswijk street. "There are mothers who give their Saint Nicolas lists to 'junkies' so that they can buy the things for half-price as presents for their families," I continued.

"Okay, okay, but not everyone is like that, Rem—only the majority."

A well-known tune from a TV series suddenly sounded in the room. Fred had been nervously switching from station to station. Our talk was over, and we didn't mind picking up the film halfway through.

CHAPTER 12

HOMELESS

Strongly threatening letters came to me from my landlord on the Torenstraat. Not that I was impressed with them, for in my thoughts I could already see myself setting their neat office on fire once the heavily built fellow came to the door. The house was going to be torn down, and everyone had to get out. And I was the first.

One evening, I came home and saw that they had ruined all the gas and water pipes. The toilet bowl had been smashed and the doors forced out of their hinges.

A good picture of how I feel inside, I thought when I saw it. "You're going to be knocked down, House," I remarked as I walked through the messed-up rooms. "Only time has a role to play, but your fate is sealed."

I could find a small room where good acquaintances lived. Of course, they were dope freaks and had just as many problems with the landlord as I did.

The floor where we three men lived was a junkyard. Everything was covered with stamped-out cigarette butts, syringe and smoking paraphernalia, and packaging from ready-to-eat-food, along with a lot of other trash. I slept with bedding on which many other people had already slept. It was damp, and there was a musty smell. We were busy the whole day trying to still our hunger for dope. If we woke up sometime late in the morning with a dizzy head, we got up and went out directly to get some more dope.

Frans, the main tenant, worked illegally, and Cees arranged various things for deliveries. You were sometimes satisfied for hours, running around town with an aggressive drive to get money in order to score. Sometimes, half was already smoked at the dealer's, and once at home, it became a whole ceremony to prepare the shot. This in itself was a sort of addiction, a kind of a kick. It became so bad that we began injecting all kinds of things—finely mashed pills mixed with water or sometimes just water. We were needle freaks, really disturbed.

Hepatitis broke out among my friends, very contagious and dangerous. Due to this and also because I didn't want to use speed anymore, I stayed away and slept here and there. Sometimes, I slept in a bus shelter or a doorway. I then injected the drugs in the open air or in the toilet of a department store or train station. I stayed for a couple of weeks in the HTO on the Rijswijkseweg. That was a good emergency solution, although it cost me sixty guilders a week, which was really very cheap in itself. But because everything always revolved around dope, I sometimes didn't even have that amount, so I had to knock around the streets again.

"Hello, Remko," an old acquaintance greeted me as I was walking through a department store.

I looked up and recognized her. "Hey, there."

She was with a girlfriend, and she looked well-groomed.

"You look good," I responded.

"Thank you," she answered, suddenly distant. "You don't . . ." She looked at her friend and began to laugh. "Now, Rem, see ya," she said and waved her hand in a disinterested way.

"Yeah, see ya," I said as they turned and went on their way. I felt insulted and dismissed. It was a hard way to discover that I must look pretty much the worst for wear.

IN JAIL

"Give me two packages," I said to the street dealer, who was also addicted and was dealing from his car. While he was giving me the packages, I saw on the side of the dealer a guy coming toward the car with a baseball bat. *He's coming to rip off this dealer*, I thought and quickly yanked the door open in order to make him go away; but with an enormous crash, the baseball bat already came smashing through the window. The attacker was like a crazy man and banged the car in quick bursts of anger. Quickly, I let myself fall out of the car and onto the stoop in an effort to get away. I suddenly heard screeching car tires behind me.

Doors swung open, and before I could react, I was caught between a knee in my back and the hood of the police car. "You can sit there for a while, boy" was the message, while the handcuffs were tightly clasped around my wrists.

Lying half on the hood, I could see how the dealer was nabbed. Spread out over the street were packages of heroine, which the dealer had quickly disposed of.

In the distance, I could see that the cops had not yet captured the guy with the baseball bat. "Nice way to rip off a dealer—with a baseball bat!"

After spending a day in the cell, I was brought to Rotterdam. In total, I was in jail four times. On the second day of my stay, the station officer came to my cell.

"And do you want to work, or would you rather sit on your butt?" he asked.

I knew that in general it would be boring work but also that you would nevertheless earn something, enough for smokes and toilet articles. The company that you had in the workplace was another advantage. "I'll work," I answered.

When I got to the workplace, I was surprised to see a familiar face. "Wooden Andre," I shouted.

"Hey, Rem, nice to see you—real nice," he said while gesturing around with his hands.

"Okay, so you're here again, I see." I laughed. "Making paper clips, I could have guessed," I said picking up the familiar board which lay on the table in front of him.

"Or putting umbrella ice cream decorations into plastic bags," he replied, nodding toward another table. "But the ice creams don't come with them," he added.

"Well, I'll make the clips," I said and sat down beside Andre.

"How long are you in for?" I asked.

"Another couple of months," he answered with a look that said that it didn't make much difference to him.

"How many of these things are we supposed to make?" I asked him.

"It doesn't matter, as long as it isn't too few."

I grabbed a couple of boxes and got to work.

"Rem," began Andre, suddenly whispering a little as if he was telling me a great secret. "Do you know why they have a girl standing by the changing rooms in the department stores these days?"

"Yes, to look in bags to see that nothing gets stolen," I answered him with a humorous look, expecting a silly answer.

"Precisely. If you've got a bag, the store personnel can ask to look in it as you leave, a routine check for stolen clothes. But I don't need a bag; I just stuff everything into my artificial leg!"

I looked at him with surprise. "Yes, of course, I hadn't thought of that." I laughed.

"The store detectives haven't either," Andre replied.

"Hey, can you get some dope smuggled in during visiting time via your wooden leg?" I suggested.

"Naturally, if you have someone who can get it and bring it in," he said.

The prison was half-full of junkies, so it could mean some good business. But we were broke, so that was that.

"Now that we can chat quietly, Andre, just how did you lose your leg?" I asked him.

"A motor accident when I was sixteen years old," he answered, threatening to sink away into his own thoughts again.

"Is this the reason you started to use dope?" I asked, now curious.

"Before I started, everyone made fun of me; but in the scene, at least I still have a bit of companionship."

I thought about his answer and saw the tragedy of it. "But what about your parents?" I threw back.

Andre waved the question aside by staring into space and mumbling something vague. I didn't ask anymore because I saw that the subject had upset him. I tried to distract him with a business question.

"Do you sell those clothes to the whores, too?"

"Yes, but I've never had a girlfriend," he said bitterly.

"Sorry, Andre, I didn't mean to upset you," I said and felt very foolish.

"Oh well, I can take that from you . . . " He waved it away from himself with a gesture as if he had cast something behind him.

Together, we made quite a lot of paper clips during the time that we were there in Rotterdam. He became a real friend, and we had a lot of fun.

I got out before Andre did. Once outside, addiction swept us away in the rapids of misery and distress. Occasionally, I came across him, but nothing came of seeing more of each other. Sometime later, he was found dead in a station toilet. The cause of his death remained vague. The depth of tragedy in his life has often given me food for thought. How very lonely he must have felt.

ON THE STREET AGAIN

After my detention, I ended up back on the street again. There were people who were so cunning as to continuously get money from the Social Services to start a "new life," but I wasn't dangerous enough, so that wasn't for me. On the street, I found all sorts of people who joined me in scoring dope. I met and mixed with all types. At a dealer's place, I met Marvin.

"Do you happen to know of a good place to pawn a fur coat?" he asked me while we sat smoking.

"Of course," I replied, smelling a profit.

"Come on, then. Let's get it right away," he said impatiently.

When we arrived at his place, he showed me a beautiful, red, fox fur coat.

"It cost at least twenty thousand," he confided in me.

"Twenty thousand," I repeated, surprised. "Where did you get it?"

"From my mother."

"Your mother . . . ?"

"Yes, it doesn't matter; she's got more than enough. How much can you get for it?"

I looked at Marvin for a moment and guessed that he wasn't yet eighteen years old.

"I don't know," I said.

"Come with me, but you'll have to wait outside."

"Okay," he answered, but when we arrived at the address of the fence, he quickly sprang inside with me. To my surprise, the fence didn't seem to mind.

This fence is rather sure of himself, I thought.

After I had pulled the red fox out of the bin bag, I laid it on the table and asked for two thousand.

"No. Eight hundred," said the dealer, bargaining disinterestedly.

"Done!" shouted Marvin, immediately interrupting us.

"You blew that deal, man," I objected.

But Marvin was in a hurry. The fence drew out a thick wad of notes and counted out the hundreds.

We bought dope with the money and prepared a shot. Amazed, I watched how Marvin dumped a whole gram onto his spoon and got it ready to shoot.

"Do you want to kill yourself?" I burst out, shocked.

"I always take this much," he said airily and gave me a boastful glance.

He's so young, I thought, and covered my eyes with my hands as he shot up. He passed out as I had expected but stayed alive.

A couple of days later in the street, an enormous Mercedes pulled up in front of me.

"Hey, Rem," called a familiar voice, and I saw Marvin sitting behind the wheel, smiling broadly. "We're going to Amsterdam, and you can drive, if you like!"

In my ragged, old clothes, I hopped in quickly. "What do your parents do, actually?" I asked him, as around one hundred miles, we passed everything that was moving on the highway to Amsterdam.

"They own more than twenty shops, even some in Belgium. But, well, I'm no businessman," he told me.

"No, I noticed that back at the fence's place," I confirmed.

"They don't have any time for me—too busy—and I guess I'm not their type. Did you know that I found out what my father's safe number is?" he said, suddenly sounding enthusiastic.

"And is there much in it?" I asked, not uninterested.

"Was, you mean. I've used it all up, actually," he said.

"That's a bit less than I was expecting," I remarked.

"And do you know what sort of punishment I got when Dad found out?" he continued.

"Well . . . "

"Staying in my room for a whole evening."

"Really? Give me a father like that. Unbelievable," I said, sitting in wonder.

In Amsterdam, we blitzed the Mercedes along the characteristic canals towards the Zeedijk. I always enjoyed Amsterdam to the fullest—the richly decorated facades of the houses along the canals, the pretty little bridges . . . A sparkling city, but alas, the scene of much grief as well.

To my annoyance, Marvin again put such an enormous amount on his spoon and lay limply on the seat beside me for the whole return journey to The Hague. It took a long time before he was able to drive the car himself again. A couple of times, I had short contact with him before losing him to an unconscious slumber once again. Years later, I heard that he had died of an overdose.

AN IMAGE

I don't know if it was a dream or if I perceived it in some other way, but it was clearly and distinctly engraved on my memory, I'm certain. I was walking in the dark on a steep cliff face. There seemed to be a large crater. I couldn't keep my footing properly on the loose ground, and I was sinking, slowly but surely, further into the depths. As I tried to fight against it, my hands couldn't get a grip on the loose earth, and every attempt to raise my leg only loosened the stones beneath me, which broke away, rumbling down into the glowing lava. Out of the depths, sulphurous gases rose from the glistening lava. Terror gripped me at the situation which I found myself in. When I looked upward despairingly for help, I experienced rather than really saw, high above me, a face which radiated fatherliness.

The expression on that face was one of intense sympathy for my hopeless situation. My heart screamed above for help, longing for deliverance. The word that at that moment, unspoken, was planted in my thoughts: "conversion."

When I came to myself, I asked myself what this could mean. What is conversion, and what did I have to do to get it? Was there, high above us, a Father Who was concerned with the joys and sorrows? I had begun to believe that there had to be a deeper reason why I was walking around on this earth. Man was surely not here to die like a worm in its own dirt.

SQUATTERS' MOVEMENT

I was still homeless, sleeping here and there. In The Paard, I got talking with someone from The Hague's squatters' movement. In general, these were people who smoked a joint and sniffed a bit of cocaine and led loose lives but kept away from heroine.

The house dealer of the subsidized Paard, who had been installed with the cooperation of The Hague's city council, possibly because of a new clause in the opium law, did good business selling his marijuana to the young people. If you used heroin, you were on the bottom rung of the ladder in the drug world. Ironically enough, it was really looked down upon. And because of this, you always tried to hide your addiction.

An exciting story was on my companion's lips.

"Yes, the municipality doesn't do anything for people with little money who are looking for accommodation, and the injustice of speculators simply leaving buildings empty should be stopped by fairer laws," he began.

I agreed with him completely.

"We've taken over an empty municipal office building. We're going to convert it into a place where young people who are looking for accommodations can live," he continued.

"It's ridiculous that you people are doing this and showing the government up for their weakness on this point," I added enthusiastically.

"Well, someone had to make a move. Otherwise, nothing happens, and many people wait up to six years for a home. We've reserved two rooms for people who, through some crisis, have become acutely homeless," he said.

"That's interesting. You people are certainly idealistic," I said thoughtfully and immediately asked him for the address.

The following day, I went straight to this address to present myself as a person in acute housing need, the victim of unscrupulous speculators. By coincidence, the squatter's committee was in session, and they could consider my request immediately.

Well, I thought, *this is certainly taking the bull by the horns once again.*

After waiting in the hall for some time, a cheerful guy came to tell me the good news that I could, indeed, have one of the two rooms reserved for this sort of situation.

"Great," I shouted, feeling really pleased. Perhaps these squatters were smarter than I had thought.

The fact that these people had got to work in an attempt to try and change society into a fairer and more just one filled me with respect for them. However, that they believed that this was possible was, in my eyes, less sensible. No one was able to change the way things went on in this world into a utopia. Call me a pessimist, if you like, but I am a realistic one. I was quite convinced about this, and no amount of discussion could change my mind. However, perhaps I would enjoy staying here. I also really wanted to know what their true motives were for working on these activities. Surely, they didn't think I was naive enough to believe that they were only full of good intentions!

"It is only for a maximum of two weeks," I was told by my host as he took me to see the room in question. "Yes, the whole idea is that there is a quick turnover. It is and should remain only a temporary, emergency solution," he said.

"Oh" came my surprised response out of a head full of thoughts.

Here we go again. "Well, we will see about that." I shrugged it off and promptly moved into the room with a girlfriend who I'd gotten to know at a friend's place and who had been an addict even longer than I had. She was the daughter of an army general.

The two weeks passed quickly, and I hadn't found any other accommodation, which wasn't surprising since I hadn't really looked and had no money to rent anyway. One morning, a pleasant squatters' leader informed me that the last day of my residence in these premises had dawned.

"But I haven't found anything else," I indignantly replied.

"I can't do anything about that," he answered.

"Then I will submit a request to extend my stay here," I said in an official manner.

The squatter saw that I was serious after considering it for a moment and said that he would bring it up at a meeting later that afternoon. So, again, I waited politely in the hall outside the meeting room. You were not allowed to participate and speak for yourself. As I waited, I began to get very annoyed. In the toilet, I tried to smoke myself into calmness, but it didn't really work.

Back in the hall, I was eaten up with thoughts of how little these squatters and their meetings differed from the municipal council, which they considered so unjust! They themselves had broken in and taken over this whole place, and now they sat reigning over it like dictators, deciding who could come in and who could not. At that moment, the leader approached me shaking his head. "No, sorry we have to keep to the principles of the policy which we have outlined . . . sorry."

This was just too much for me, and I snapped at him that he would do better to go back and tell the meeting that the whole building must be evacuated tonight.

"Why evacuated?" he asked flabbergasted.

"Because tonight, flames and a jerrycan full of gasoline will be hurled in through a window, stupid!" I growled.

He must have seen from my face that I really meant it, as he turned around and hurried back to the meeting. Absolutely beside myself, I began to pace up and down while all sorts of images of just how I could wreck the place flashed through my brain.

After a very short time, the leader returned, calling down the hall. "Okay, okay, you can stay for another two weeks, but you will have to look for other accommodations soon!"

"You know what?" I said to him threateningly. "I've made a decision. I'm going to stay here just as long as I find it necessary."

Furious, I returned to my room. "Even so, when I do leave here, I'll still set fire to the whole thing," I raved on to my girlfriend.

"Ah, let it be," she said as she tried to hush me.

"You are only interested in your own affairs," I reproached her, irritated. Everything irritated me, and it took a while before things had cooled down again.

In any case, the squatters had taught me that there were more possibilities to get a house than just through the official channels. Besides, my brother Rik's house in Spoorwijk was empty. I looked at it now with other eyes. An empty house . . . while I was homeless? A crowbar was quickly found, and together with an acquaintance, I demolished the back door to become a squatter in that house.

Here and there, I managed to collect some furniture and stayed inside for the required forty-eight hours. After forty-eight hours' occupation, you could not be put out of a dwelling without a lot of legal fuss. In the first weeks, there was no sign from either the municipality, the house organization, or the police.

CHAPTER 13

TRIP

It was around that time that I had a peculiar experience. One of those deep impressions that I can still remember so clearly.

I hadn't really been around in the time that LSD, a strong hallucinogen, was "in." But here were still the so-called "trips" for sale. If you wanted them, they were there to be found, and there were plenty of wild stories going around about what was experienced during these trips.

These were stories about drug-users of a generation before mine. Of flower-power and hippie-time. My older sister had had a head-start on me there, literally tripping on hashish and witch's salve. At one point, I saw her wandering around in long skirts made from tablecloths and a bag full of weeds, which you weren't supposed to call weeds anymore because of their supposed healing properties and substitutes for insecticides, repelling all sorts of unwanted insects indoors and outside.

I got to know one of these old freaks. Looking like a prophet with shoulder-length hair, he lit up one joint after the other. Although he held extensive dissertations on philosophy and the meaning of life, on the practical level, you gained very little from him. Not because of lack of talent but simply because he was too musty to move about. Like so many other users, he had also developed trouble with his digestive system and, as a result, sometimes sat on the toilet for hours.

Once, he asked me to help him move. Arriving at the house with a few acquaintances, we began loading up the moving truck. Halfway down the stairs, he decided that he needed to go to the toilet and proceeded to take an hour-long break for this operation. Perhaps in his "enlightened state," he imagined that he had helped load up the truck. However, he joined us just as we were placing the last of his possessions in the truck. Setting a chair down on the pavement, he sat down and, with a satisfied smile, said how great it had been that the move had been done so quickly. Thus, my image of trip-freaks was not very positive.

The well-known stories about people on "trips" who imagined they could fly and, under that delusion, stepped out of windows eleven stories up were not totally made up, I felt sure. What is also well-known is that many young people landed themselves in deep psychological problems through taking LSD and other hallucinogens, such as the over-use of hashish. Many began to suffer from phobias and frightening voices. Some became totally possessed.

I soon realized that with "trips," you really had to watch out!

Even so, I did once take a "trip." In fact, I had already come to the point where I was using everything. Too much alcohol, cocaine, speed, and heroine. In a particularly careless mood, I could find myself doing things which set off alarm bells ringing deep inside me. The drugs themselves made you feel heedless and go over limits which you would have preferred to respect. Those were dangerous moments.

Someone came to me with "trips." They were very mild and pleasant trips, he assured me. It was on a weekend, and I was just about to go out dancing. It was a beautiful, clear night, the perfect one to experience something special!

Rather excited, I took the "trip" and left a little while later for the Paard in downtown Hague. On the way, the trip started to work, and I began to experience everything differently, including colors and sounds. I saw everything with "other" eyes. It was very hard to describe.

When I arrived at The Paard, a friend pressed a beer into my hand. My attention was drawn to the surging movement of the mass of people on the dance floor. It was very busy that evening. I noticed that there were a lot of weirdly dressed punks among the swinging crowd. The music was, as always, loud and intrusive rock. I just stood there as if glued to the spot, only able to stare—all those punks and freaks, the smoke and swirling lights, the moving sea of people whipped up by the fast drum rhythm.

As if I were looking through a tele-lens that could be turned to make things become sharper, I began to distinguish horrible shapes in the shadows of the spectacle—demonic figures which seemed to increase in number and size. They seemed pleased with what was going on. With their black, scaly arms and clawed hands, they made grinning, encouraging gestures to the crowd. Their jaws, dripping with saliva, were grinning possessively, like hungry beasts who already have their victims within their power. I saw that most of the individuals in the crowd were connected to dark rays that went out from these horrid creatures.

The intuitive thought came to my mind that these devilish powers were busy with a pre-arranged plan to bind people, to urge them on to further stupidities, which would lead to the ruining of their young lives, so that they could finally take complete possession of them and torture them. At that moment, I heard a witchlike laugh resound and was pierced to my depths by the shocking thought that I also had been caught in their sticky web for a long time.

In that same moment, an enormous rage against these horrors took over me. Like a reflex, I threw the beer glass that I had been holding in my hand all this time at the enemies in the shadows. The glass must have ended up in the middle of the people on the dance floor. Blind with rage, I picked up empty beer glasses that were within my reach and threw them at the scornful demons.

While I was doing all this in my blind frenzy, someone pulled me aside with an enormous wrench. I tried as hard as I could to pull away but didn't get very far. With a second powerful wrench, I was led away through chaos until I could feel cold air acting upon my body and saw the familiar historic facades of the Prinsegracht appearing.

"Get yourself together, will you? Are you out of your mind!" I heard a familiar voice screaming. Taken aback, I came to my senses and looked into the outraged face of my friend.

"If the doorman had seen you, he would have smashed your face in, you idiot!" He glared at me.

"Hey, wait a minute, you palmed this bad trip off on to me, remember?" I said, suddenly piecing it all together.

Later, my friend told me that he had watched me swearing like a maniac and throwing empty beer glasses all over the place. He had taken the initiative to haul me out of the Paard before the door could do that in his special way. I was very thankful that he had prevented my face from having to be totally rebuilt! Those who knew the strong hand of the doorman knew what I meant.

Nevertheless, I'd had the rude awakening that it is better to get slammed by a doorman than to remain bound by those dark forces. My mate had saved me just in time from the doorman's shove, but who could still save me from the power of those invisible soul-eaters from the shadows?

EEF

I had a couple of visitors, and one began speaking about Eef.

"Hey, that ex of yours has really got herself lost, eh?" I looked at him a bit distrustfully. Eef was a sensitive subject with me, and if I heard negative reports about her here and there, I quickly felt anger rising in me.

"How's that?" I asked. "Now, that guy she's with sometimes beats her black and blue. That man has no sense . . ." As he was saying that, I was seeing him beating her in my thoughts and felt an enormous anger and hate rising up in me.

"Where are they staying?" I asked.

"I believe that her cousin has beaten the guy up and that she's away from him now," he told me.

That calmed my temper down a little, and I stared ahead of me.

"I remember that cousin. He lives in California and visits the Netherlands from time to time—a good guy and enormously strong physically, good worker," I said while lost in thought. I was working out a way I might be able to get in contact with Eef again.

From that moment on, I asked here and there, trying to know her whereabouts. A few people could give me some vague information, but Bernard, a mutual friend of Eef's and mine, came up with something clearer. He saw me walking in the street and came directly to me.

"Hey, Rem," he called to me from the opposite side of the street.

When I looked up, I saw a laughing face; I could see that things were going well with him. At least, he was looking healthy.

"Good to see ya. How are things?" I asked.

"Swell, going great, and you?" he asked straight away as we began to walk together.

"Could be better, but . . . well, you know how things are . . . Have you heard anything of Eef?" I said, not wanting to talk about myself.

"Yes, actually, quite a lot . . . " he trailed off.

I looked at him. "Now, tell me quickly then . . . "

"Listen," he began. "It just kept getting worse with her. She kept using more cocaine, heroin, and pills all mixed up together, and she looked terrible in the end . . . Then, she had a really nasty experience and attempted suicide," he continued, looking at me earnestly.

"A suicide attempt?" I repeated, astounded. "That isn't like Eef!"

"No, but you know the sort of things that can happen on the street," he said and gave me a meaningful look.

"Yeah . . . "

To be addicted as a man was one thing, but as a woman, it was a direct disaster. Used and misused by everyone, like being delivered over to the wolves. Don't tell me anything about respectable gentlemen who have to go out on the lunch break or have to drop by a friend for a while in the evening or stay on late at work and then get robbed, threatened, beaten, and cast off.

"She tried it with pills. More than twenty-seven Isonoxen and also Rophynol—enough, in any case, to fell a horse—but to everyone's astonishment, she came around in the hospital."

I listened to all of this with a sick feeling. "How is she now?" I asked curiously.

"Well, when she came to, she was extremely angry that it hadn't worked and that she had to keep on living in this rotten world."

"I can imagine," I said, understanding.

"How do you know about all this anyway?" I asked him.

"Well, the good news is that Eef has been in a rehabilitation center in Amsterdam called the Heil des Volks, a Christian organization, and it's really going well with her."

"Oh," I replied in surprise.

"Your mother had that address of a Christian rehab center in Amsterdam," he said.

"Yes, and you went there, and I even wrote to you there," I said, finishing his thought for him.

"Not only that but you said that you wished that I could let Eef know about the center, and I did."

"And now she's there, too!" I blurted out, more amazed than skeptical.

"Through Eef's mother, who bribed her by promising to make her a suede coat if she would go there. And after the suicide attempt and all the other distress, Eef took her up on it."

"And now, she's there," I filled in for him again.

"Yes," he said optimistically.

"Unbelievable, and we've all had a part in it." I repeated this news a couple of times, considering it.

"You should go there, too, Rem," he began to tell me.

"That is my decision to make. Just see that you keep on the right track yourself. Anyway, what are you doing here in town?" I asked, looking at him suspiciously.

"Weekend leave. It feels great to be clean and wandering through town," he said, totally happy. My suspicions turned into jealously. We talked some more before parting. The knowledge that Eef was in the rehab center did me a whole lot of good.

CHAPTER 14

TRYING TO GET CLEAN

WHO WANTS TO BE A JUNKIE?

No one wants to be a junkie. Ask one, and he or she will invariably tell you about the many times he or she has tried to kick the habit. You can get clean, but staying clean is another matter. Every time I tried to kick the habit, I did it because I'd had enough and because of the awful misery I saw that drugs caused in people's lives, including my own.

COLD TURKEY

Sleepless nights; first hot, then cold sweats; a continuous gnawing pain in the nerves of my legs; along with depression and apathy. During the period you're trying to get clean, you're plagued with strong temptations and an intense longing for dope. Each hour you could stay clean was a gain, each day a victory. The sleepless nights that you lay twisting and turning in bed seemed to last forever.

You had to get through almost one week before the withdrawal symptoms went away and the coveted sleep came back. Many times, I made such an attempt, and sometimes, I got through it; but usually, I gave up halfway through. The moment that you gave up, you felt a weight falling off you. You could again enter the stream of addiction. To keep going meant having to fight, and obviously, it was a very hard fight.

The awful experience that the "trip" gave was a reason to try to get out of the claws of addiction yet again. In the meantime, I lived free of charge, as no one came to collect the rent. I knew from the neighbors that the rents were very low.

"Now, if no one comes to me, then I'll go to them," I reasoned. Not because I was afraid that the police, with their renowned water cannon, would hose me out of the house but because I began to long for order and regularity in my life.

"Good chance that you'll be given it," the neighbor egged me on when I talked to him about it.

"It's not such a great neighborhood," he continued.

"So, there are possibilities," I finished off his sentence.

I didn't find the neighborhood a problem, but then I probably had lower standards than he did. Through some detective work, I found an employee of the city of The Hague to talk to about the house I had moved into.

"How can someone get clean if he doesn't have a roof over his head?" I asked him. I received permission to live in the house.

Immediately, I began to fix the house up. My drug habit was a hindrance. I decided that what I had to do was kick the habit and get rid of drugs for good.

KICK THE HABIT WITH ALCOHOL

In the scene, it was said that you could kick the drug habit with alcohol, strong sleeping pills, or tranquilizers to cut down the effects of stopping. Drinking appealed to me. One time, blind drunk on wine, I reeled through the room where the walls were turning around, as if I was on a Ferris wheel that had gone out of control. That was nice, and I laughed myself sick over nothing; but after a while, the Ferris wheel began to turn faster and faster. I wanted to get off, but the operator, with a sneering laugh, made it go even faster.

The sleep that I got from this method of kicking the habit was, according to my advisers, more a case of being unconscious. After a couple of days, I got a terrible headache and felt so awful that I thought getting clean this way was like a form of dying.

WITH METHADONE

Some time ago, the methadone programs were introduced. *Maybe this is the answer,* I thought at the time. A scheme to limit the withdrawal symptoms to a minimum.

I reported to the CAD on the Brouwersgracht in The Hague. After a talk with a social worker, I was given a permanent number: 682. With this number, I got ten drops of methadone and was to work in a system of reducing this dose by one drop every two days.

I met up with addicts who just grabbed the whole bottle of methadone out of the hands of the program assistants. Since methadone is an opiate, it has the same effect on a junkie as honey has on a bee. Now, I noticed, as a result, they had made bars and a sliding hatch where they gave out the methadone. Hardly anyone becomes permanently clean by using methadone. In the beginning, there was a bit of idealism behind distributing it, and it was in that period that I joined the program. I was motivated then. I had really had enough of the addiction, and the fact that I now had good ground floor living accommodation strengthened my motivation. I went through the methadone withdrawal system according to the rules.

After I had taken the last drop, I was quite sick, but I was used to that by now, and I knew that I would get through it. I was, therefore, a success case for the program and the program assistants, who incidentally were well-meaning people and very happy for me.

The real problem came after I was clean. But this time, I had developed a good plan; and now that I had a home, it had to work. It was spring. I began fixing up my house and doing volunteer work. Together with another person, I was allowed to establish the *Spoor Neighborhood Newspaper,* make the layout, write up interviews, go to the printer, and deliver the paper.

An acquaintance introduced me to surfboarding. I bought a second-hand board and made it my hobby—it was both healthy and sporty.

Still, something was missing. This all changed when I met a very nice young lady. She was a nurse and had never had anything to do with drugs, just what I needed.

Through her, I came into contact once again with the "other world," the world of "clean" people. That summer was a success story for me, and I felt that all was well. Financially, I had finally enough money to get my driving license.

During the driving exam, I made a bad mistake, but the examiner was sympathetic to my story. I had convinced him of the importance of getting my license quickly so that I would have a better chance of getting a job and be able to re-integrate into the community. And I really meant it. I bought an old second-hand car for a couple of hundred guilders, and for the first time, I felt the peace of being able to drive around with a license and insurance.

It was great! I fought against getting back into drugs by drinking an extra beer. A few months passed. The summer was over, and I began to think seriously if it wasn't time for me to join the working force again. Certainly, I now had everything: a house, a girlfriend, a car, and work—volunteer, but nevertheless, a way to use my time well. Why did I still have deep inside me a feeling that something was missing?

On weekends, I went out and drank more than usual, but where was the fullness of life? I was bothered by a dissatisfied feeling deep inside me. I shared this with my girlfriend, but she couldn't understand it.

She had her own worries and things out of her past to work through. She took me to meet her parents, and it was very nice, but I didn't really feel any attachment. It was all loose sand. After hanging around in the "clean" world, I understood that "clean" was a very relative thing. There were drinkers, pill poppers, workaholics, neurotics, and partygoers—the men who read sex books and the women gossip magazines. Oh, I knew it—all of us were lost. What I had read in my mother's books, I could see all around me. Without God, the godless know there is no rest. I was worried about my girlfriend; women often had a really awful life in this world, I thought, and what could she do with such a mixed-up character as I was? I began to feel guilty about her.

One beautiful day, I was returning from Noordwijk, where I had been surfing, and now, I came into The Hague via the Rijksstraatweg. Like a streak of lightning on a clear day, a complete mental breakdown hit me. Suddenly, I could no longer see the point in struggling any further. Why should I? It was very disappointing—the "clean" life, what an emptiness it all was. There was also an enormous emptiness inside me. I had a wallet full of money, and I pictured giving myself a treat with a large shot of heroine.

I tried to fight against it by telling myself that anything was better than heroin. It was like an awful claw had hold of me and had such power over me that I was almost powerless to stand up to it. The craving for dope was terribly strong.

"Don't do it," I said to myself, but the pressure remained, and the surrender came when I shrugged my shoulders and gave in. Within a few minutes, I was at the door of a dealer, and the moment I got the first whiff, I couldn't have cared less.

The following day, I woke up sick and knew that all my efforts had ended in failure.

My relapse was both sharp and deep. Within the shortest time, I was using a lot every day. I told my girlfriend that it was better that we split up to protect her from the same misery.

A BIBLE AND NEEDLE

One day, my mother came to visit me in the Spoorwijk. I hadn't the faintest idea if she knew about my life. According to me, she had no idea how shaky it was. She gave me a book as a present. She did that more often, but this time, the book was the Bible itself—a traditional, black State Translation. As if it were holiness itself, it was placed on the table, and that is where it lay.

Sometimes, I read it, and many things were difficult to understand because of the language used in that particular translation.

However, from the text, I understood that everyone would be held responsible for his deeds in this world and that everyone had to come before the throne of God. Those who had led a bad life would be thrown into Hell, but those who followed Jesus on the road to peace would be given everlasting life. As for the future, I was getting more anxious than ever.

As it was, neither the present nor future life in this world seemed so great, so to have to anticipate an even darker eternity as well . . . ! When I learned that, I tried to act cool, but deep inside me, the doubt was growing whether it could really be true.

I certainly wasn't the country's greatest citizen. I was willing to admit that, but I wasn't all bad either—things had just sort of come out that way.

Sometimes, the table was full of junkie paraphernalia and needles, a strange sight next to the Bible. Friends regularly asked me what that book was doing there. I had also read that you shouldn't talk to a fool because he would despise the wisdom of wise words. That was the proverb that my mother had written in the front of the Bible, and I knew it by heart.

Still, I gave an honest answer and discovered that it applied more to me than I was willing to admit. I even began to see it as completely just and fair that in the end, everyone must bear responsibility for what he did on earth.

As far as I could see, most people couldn't care less about God and His commandments. Everyone lived according to his own ideas and not God's. More and more, I began to understand how human history had left a trail of blood and why the world was in such a mess.

I wanted to change things, but how? The problem was within me; how could I get rid of it? Just like the day that an acquaintance sprawled out on the couch, stoned, another was getting a syringe ready, and I was "chinesing."

"What book is that?" asked Rene.

"A Bible," I answered.

"Do you read it?" Rene asked with interest.

"Not much, but there are a couple of things that I know," I replied.

"One thing is sure, though. We junkies are going to Hell."

"Oh, you're a cheerful fellow," remarked Rene with a laugh.

"Yeah, we go around robbing and stealing, don't we? Now then, how are we going to look standing before the throne of God? Where everything is known and nothing is hidden from Him,, and you're punished if you have broken His law . . . so what the police here below don't get you for, is punished up above," I heard myself earnestly preaching.

"Then you better stay here for a few more years," joked Rene.

"Yeah, laugh about it, but you better pray for forgiveness," I went on preaching. I had to admit that I could sometimes ruin the mood with my sermons, but they didn't see that I myself was the one who was most bothered.

"So, you're going to Hell, too, Remko," Rene thoughtfully concluded.

"It sure is a problem." I told them that, at night, I prayed for forgiveness. I often had difficulties with my own spirituality and couldn't get to sleep because of it.

Many times, I decided to stop, but the next day the craving took over again. And so, I went on my well-worn way back to the dealer to get the much-needed dope.

Between the addict's paraphernalia, the cigarette butts, and other stuff on the table lay the Bible. What a contradiction! Even though I tried to limit my use of drugs as much as possible, things still went wrong. Once, in the middle of the day, I was shocked to come to and realize that I had been out with a burning cigarette in my hand. The butt had burned deep into my thigh, and I hadn't felt a thing!

THE CRIMINAL

During that time, I read a book that my mother had once been given. What I read had stayed in my mind. It concerned the death of Christ. He was nailed to a cross with a criminal on His right and one on His left. The Roman soldiers gambled for the clothes of the men on the crosses. Some onlookers jeered at Him, along with one of the men being crucified. But what really struck me was that the criminal being crucified on His right hand side was annoyed with all the jeering. He reprimanded the jeerer by saying that he and the other man were indeed guilty but that Jesus was not guilty. Jesus was innocent.

Then he turned to Christ and humbly asked Him to remember him when He was in His kingdom. Jesus' answer surprised me: "Today you will be with me in paradise." *What a forgiveness*, I thought. The criminal couldn't make it right anymore with the people whom he had hurt. He was forgiven, not because he could justify himself but because he had humbled himself and asked Christ to remember him in Heaven.

I was jealous of the criminal. He was in paradise! What we were all seeking, He was given with his last breath.

"Oh, if only I could just live in a small corner of that paradise," I wished aloud. But what did this mean to me, and how would that word "saved" apply to me? I simply didn't know. The days passed, and my addiction kept me in its iron grip.

One night, I suddenly woke up and prayed to God, trusting that He heard my prayer. I asked Him what I must do to be saved. Some days later, I got a strong feeling that I should leave The Hague and make a new start with my mother in Goes. From this strong compulsion, I understood that this was the answer to my question.

I had to leave everything behind—give up my house, my girlfriends, my loose and undisciplined lifestyle with all its fleshly desires—and no longer be able to do what I felt like and begin trying to lead a good life? At the age of twenty-five, living in a room in my mother's home again was something that didn't appeal to me at all. I fought against the idea. On the one hand, I didn't want to ruin myself any further. On the other hand, I had trouble with the idea that God was merciful but that at the same time He also pointed the way toward obedience. Somewhere deep inside me, I longed for an instant solution—maybe a pill or a flash of lightning or something like that—which would give me the healing I wanted without my having to work too hard to get it.

It was a difficult choice, wrestling with myself. Would I have to give up control, not follow my own will, beliefs, or ways? Would God determine my way?

CHAPTER 15

ACCIDENT

In addition to using drugs, I also drank a lot. I stole bottles of sherry from the liquor store and spent whole evenings half-stoned and half-drunk with my earphones on, laying on the couch or looking at the television. The struggle went on, and I delayed making a radical change; I just couldn't do it. One evening while watching a film on TV, I drank a whole bottle of wine. An acquaintance had introduced me to a dealer who "puffed." When the film was over, I decided to go to his place.

Half-drunk, I drove over. When I came in, he was "basing." That was a new way to smoke cocaine—with a waterpipe. You got a sharp jolt from it, and that felt great. However, that feeling only lasted for a short time, leaving the typical after-effect, when it seemed to turn on you and give you a feeling of intense emptiness. The result was that you wanted to "base" again as quickly as possible.

That's the way it was some nights, and because the drug took away your appetite, you looked as though you were fading away, so to speak, by the hour. To fill up the emptiness, I took heroine after "basing." Owing more than one hundred guilders to my dealer, I got in my car and went home. I found myself moving in slow motion, which wasn't unpleasant. It felt more like being on a luxury cruise ship sailing on a calm sea . . . until there was a loud crash. Slowly, the feeling began to come back into my body.

Half-conscious, laying on the ground, I focused on the veins in the asphalt, a thousand little roads. Saliva drooled out of my mouth. My body felt heavy as lead, and I had no control over my muscles, which didn't bother me at all. I let my spirit freely endure this experience. Nothing mattered at all. I was alone, flat on the ground, one with the earth. I was in such close contact with the earth that I felt a part of it.

Strange, but I had kind of a trusting relationship with the street. The street has something reliable about it. Other things come and go, but the street remains more or less the same. I had drifted over and around the street for so much of my life.

Vaguely, I could feel my swollen hand, and I heard someone very far away say, "Lay him at the side of the road."

Suddenly, I registered crackling leather right next to me, and vague shapes became sharper as they turned into a pair of brown, leather, newly polished shoes.

I tried to move. With some effort, I stretched my neck to look up and saw the trouser legs of a cop. Between the shoes, I could see my car in the distance, upside down and right across the street. There were people around me, of course.

"That's my car." I suddenly realized.

"Stand up," said a bass voice. With some difficulty, I scrambled up.

"Do you have pain anywhere?" asked the cop.

I cautiously brushed off my trousers and didn't feel anything. "I don't think so," I answered honestly.

"Good, get into the car then," he said with routine coolness.

This cop was also sick and tired of all the junkies—always trouble, hopeless, I had to admit to myself. But everyone is in the grip of something—drugs, perversion, money, power, career, possessions.

Why me again? I thought crossly. Everything flashed through my mind there in the police car.

Why didn't I have any control over my life? Some people had everything under control, or so it seemed. They knew how to make things work. They knew what buttons to turn at what time, and they were in control of what was going on. Or did it just seem so? In any case, I knew didn't have any control. I was thrown back and forth like a buoy in the waves. Someone pulled me up and pushed me out. Greater powers, though I didn't know who or what.

Later, I heard that I had driven from the wrong direction into a traffic island with an emergency lane. Just then, someone was backing out of a parking place, and I crashed into him, then turned over and side-swiped and damaged four parked cars. A person who saw the accident had pulled me out of my car through the broken back window and laid me on the street.

The police were there quickly because it happened right across from the station. The first letter I got from the insurance company that week contained the information that I had been immediately taken off their records. The police had taken a blood test, but surprisingly enough, I got my driving license back because I was not over the legal amount. The cocaine had probably neutralized the liquor in my blood. When I later examined my car, I was surprised that I had survived the crash without even a scratch. Did guardian angels exist? I was convinced that God had protected me.

After the accident, I felt guilty and empty and very addicted. I also felt a big, gaping hole inside myself. I absolutely did not want to be an addict, but I had no say about it; like a galley slave in olden times, I had to continue. The relentless and merciless master whipped the slaves in his chosen direction and in his service. I recognized my powerlessness. All the time that I was stealing things from stores, I felt guilty and rotten.

I was only twenty-five years old, but I was washed out. Nothing had any taste or value. I wanted to break with my past and purify it. Only a Greater Power, a Higher Authority than the slave driver, could help me. This situation went on for weeks.

OLD COAT

One afternoon, I looked around me while I was lying on the couch and saw the things I had collected, the surfboard that still hung in the hall, the paintings which I had made from time to time and were now displayed around the house.

I thought about girls that I had been involved with in the past months. They didn't know what to do with their lives either, and I recognized a lot of myself in them. The purpose of their relationships was mainly mutual consolation.

"Soon, I'll also have it on my conscience that, because of me, they got on the dope," I thought. My coat hung on the back of the chair. It was a classical style, black and made of very thick pig skin. It was a code sign in certain circles. It said something like: "I'm a freak; I'm with the times." I had bought the thing a couple of years before. It was thrown over the back of the chair, and I sat there for a while, staring at it.

If I sell that stupid thing, then I'll be able to buy a train ticket to Goes, and I can start over again; it's time for a new coat, anyway, I thought. It was a symbol of my choice. I was going to Goes. I surrendered.

Charging just a small amount for taking it over, I was quickly rid of the house—there were plenty of people looking for a place to live.

CHAPTER 16
MIRACLE WEEK

Naturally, my mother was pleased that I had come. What can you do without a mother? My stepfather had always acted in a friendly way; and he showed his hospitality this time as well, although in the past, he had had to make some major adjustments because of us. Arguments, police at the door, problems at school—you name them, we had them. When I arrived in Goes, I decided to go cold turkey. That wasn't the worst thing to have to go through, and yet, everything developed differently from what I had expected or imagined. That week, the local Christian churches had organized a tent campaign. The second day that I was in Goes, I suddenly decided to help set up the tent. Even though I didn't feel so good, it was better to keep moving and to get to know people right away. The following day, the spectacle was going to begin, and I was curious what it was going to be like.

That evening, there were two speakers. First, music, and then a long sermon. I didn't understand very much of it. At the end of the sermon, people who wanted to be converted were invited to come forward. I thought that I was converted already. *I've been converted from The Hague to Goes, and that is quite a change,* I thought.

The pastor continued, saying that people who wanted to receive strength in order to stay in their Christian life could come forward for prayer. That invitation greatly appealed to me because I realized that I could never be saved all by myself. Maybe, with the best of intentions, I could hold out for a few weeks. A junkie has a third eye for dope; he sees directly where and to whom he has to go.

I also went forward in Goes. I was taken to a tent behind the big tent, and two pastors laid their hands on my shoulders and began to pray out loud for me.

One of the pastors said, "The Lord says, 'Child, know that I will never more abandon you.'"

At that moment, I experienced God's forgiveness, which was given to me through belief in Jesus. I could only kneel and feel grateful. Joyfully, I went home.

The next day, however, I was sick as a dog. I had terrible diarrhea and kept throwing up, to the point that I thought my stomach was coming up as well. I thought that it was the devil playing around with me. I had promised my mother that I would wash her car, and in spite of how I felt, I started on it. I couldn't go on very long, however. Soon, I was back in bed, tossing and turning, with a pail to puke in beside me. This went on until the evening when I fell asleep from fatigue.

In the middle of the night, I woke up singing, with an overpoweringly good feeling. Out of my mouth came sounds telling of God's greatness, an experience that was completely new to me. In my mind, I couldn't explain this phenomenon, but I didn't fight against it—just the opposite. I felt intuitively that God was at work. The phenomenon lasted several hours before I again fell asleep. The next day, I felt clean and reborn. I experienced a deep peace and happiness and knew what I had missed and had been looking for. Jesus was indeed the risen Prince of Peace about Whom it was always sung at Christmas!

I had never expected that He could make Himself known with such power. He was it—Jesus Christ! This was the Power I had prayed for, and for the first time, I really believed that things would turn out all right for me.

Now I understood that conversion was not the difference between doing good things and bad things but between being focused on Him or on something else. Christ had to be at the center. I couldn't believe that you first received so much forgiveness and then, on top of that, received such inner fulfillment. It was fantastic!

Never again have I had doubts about Jesus. He was my God and my Friend. I knew that I still had a lot to learn, but He would be with me. My mother and Johan, my stepfather, were in seventh heaven because of what happened. They had prayed so much for me, and now they saw the answer to their prayers. When I played sports that week, I noticed that I had breath. Because of the drugs and smoking over the past ten years, going up a couple of stairs was "condition training" for me. My lungs felt bad if I took a deep breath. And now? I really felt clean there, too. The sick day must have been a complete, physical cleaning out. The surprising thing about it, too, was that I no longer felt like smoking.

Since then, I haven't touched the "stink sticks" again; the desire was taken away. Later that week, I saw just how amazing God's plan was. The day after the experience, the telephone rang.

My mother said, "Yes, he's here," and of course told the good news about me. "Here he is," she said as she handed me the telephone.

It was Eef! I still loved her. However, I didn't give her time to say anything but told once more what had happened to me.

"And," I blurted out, "also, I don't need you anymore because Jesus is now Number One."

Eef stood in the phone booth playing with coins, and just as the last second tone sounded, she interrupted me and said, "Yes, but I love you."

"I love you, too," I yelled back.

The next day, I barreled down as fast as I could in Mum's car to Groningen where Eef was in an addiction withdrawal/rehabilitation farmhouse. We fell into each other's arms. It was all quite unbelievable.

It was really special seeing one another again. We took a long walk over the wide meadows in the Groningen countryside.

"Rem, I have something to tell you. You know, when I went to that center in Amsterdam to kick the drugs, I had a medical examination. It appeared that I was pregnant, and that shocked me; and I had a terrible time because I didn't know who the father could be, and I didn't know how it had happened. Normally, I would get an abortion, but now I was conscience-stricken because of my belief. First, at evening prayers, I had laughed mockingly about belief and the Bible and the hallelujah songs that we sang. I could hardly control myself. I believed more in evolution and that sort of thing.

"But nevertheless, I gradually began to experience something. I had an enormous battle within myself, and I was forced to make a choice. It was just as if God spoke to me and told me that I had to choose—for the past, death, drugs, my own way, and thus also for an abortion—or for the new life, being clean, going God's way, and thus not destroying the new life inside me. I had a terribly hard time and had to fight my confusing thoughts.

"At a certain moment, after a Sunday service, God's Word spoke to my heart, and that evening, I got down on my knees in my bedroom and prayed to God to choose life. At that moment, I felt a big weight of hate, revenge, rejection, and helplessness fall off me, and a heavenly peace and joy came into my heart in its place. It was really great, and through this experience, I realized that God really lives and loves and is interested in people and longed to help me, too.

"From then on, I have become a real Christian, and I am so thankful that God has taken on my sins. Although I can hardly understand how it all works, I have surrendered myself, and I already see the new life.

"You know, naturally the fruit blows away, but the inner peace has stayed with me."

"Praise the Lord," I said as I hugged Eef. "He has brought us together again. Marvelous."

And we enjoyed the happiness that warmed our hearts.

"How come you called me?" I asked, now that we were so familiar with one another again.

"Now," she began to joke, "when I was in the second phase here at the farm in Groningen for a few months, I began to long for a man, and I thought, yeah, a nice, rich farm guy and living in the country really attracts me."

I looked at her thoughtfully. "Go on," I said.

"Well, I prayed for this."

"For a man?" I asked while giving her an appraising look.

"Yeah, why not? God knows everything, and you can pray about everything but when I did that, your name came into my mind."

"Good thinking," I said jokingly.

"Yeah, but you were still a junkie in The Hague," she shot back.

"Oh, thanks a lot, but go on, " I said, and she continued.

"After a few weeks of doubting and uncertainty, I thought about calling your mother and asking how you were—and you know the rest."

"Exactly in my miracle week. Unbelievable," I replied.

We ended our visit with the agreement that we would have an old-fashioned engagement, and it took place that same month.

ON THE BOAT

The week after that remarkable week, I was practicing drumming when I saw a boy come into our front garden. He put a folder in our mailbox. The folder was an invitation for a youth evangelization meeting on an inland water boat.

I called at once and said that I could help. During the boat evangelization campaign, I met new people. The fun and solidarity, but also the pure purpose of the team doing this work, greatly appealed to me. One evening in old Beyerland, I gave my testimony to an overly filled boat, telling about the ups and downs in my life and what had so recently happened to me. For the first time, I experienced how God could work though me to give hope to others. In the first two weeks after my conversion, I was able, through prayer, to lead two people to Christ. I realized that missionary work was high on God's priority list. He sent His Son to save and appointed the saved to be missionaries.

The campaign gave me new friends and a vision for the future. But this did not mean that I forgot about my earthly life.

Within a month, I had organized a real old-fashioned engagement party for Eef and me. We had a very nice garden party with the new friends I had met in the Christian community and during the boat trip.

CONTINUING PEACE?

The Lord is the Spirit, and where the Spirit of the Lord is, there is freedom. I read this in the Bible and also experienced it.

I still enjoyed the great inner freedom that I had fallen into. The gaping emptiness in me was gone. I hadn't the vaguest idea of what I would do—work or take a course—but one thing I did know was that life was not meaningless. I often asked myself if the inner rest would go away and if it would all cool down. Perhaps it was only a sort of light wave that at a certain moment reached its peak, then diminished and finally flowed away to an unknown place. My happiness would then be of a temporary nature. Must it be that way? One moment of enlightenment, and then live the rest of your life on the basis of that short experience?

I read in the Bible that somewhere out on the street, Jesus called to the people, "From those who believe in me, as it says in the scriptures, will flow streams of living water from within. This said God of the Holy Spirit which all those who believe in Him will receive."

When I was a drug addict, I didn't understand much of what I read in the Bible, but now, suddenly, much more of what I read was becoming clear, although a lot of questions still remained. But I didn't let that bother me.

From this text, I understood that inner peace flows out of the source of life, a source that would never dry up! Much better than a million in the bank or a harem of women!

In fact, I now understood that all the earthly things put together could not satisfy the deepest spiritual needs. All the money in the world could not buy inner joy. On the contrary, to my mind, this was the only way to be cured of the pursuit of money, women, drugs, power, and other such things, which in fact derive from restlessness, spiritual emptiness and identity problems. The pursuer and the pursued were past—hunting season was over. The power of sin and, thereby, the power of the big hunter, the devil and his demonic creatures, had lost their hold on me. My sins were forgiven, and I had to make sure that it stayed that way. No more forbidden fruit, sweet in the mouth for a very short time but oh-so-bitter and sour in the stomach.

A good marriage, having and bringing up children and remaining faithful and being a good father, working for your living, and being a positive person in society remain something very worthwhile. I still didn't know that there was much more possible in the Kingdom of God than there is in this world. All the injustice, yes, I had trouble with that, too. Why? Why must things happen in such awful ways? The only Person without sin was crucified when He was just thirty-three years old.

Fortunately, I now fully realized why, and I decided to tell others about it, also as a way to let others see that there is a way—a wholesome way—a way that perhaps is not always easy, but one which leads to Heaven, praise God!

Oh, I couldn't care less that people would laugh at me as a hallelujah freak. I would not hide my faith, regardless of what people would say about it.

CHAPTER 17

APOLOGIES

In the beginning weeks, I read the Bible and thought about things. For the first time, I read the familiar Lord's Prayer in the Bible itself: "Forgive us our debts as we forgive our debtors."

Suddenly, the thought came to me to ask the forgiveness of people that I had, to put it mildly, in large or small measure harmed by the way I had lived. I was shocked at this thought, especially when I realized the number of people I had actually hurt throughout the years and whom I owed! I pushed the thought away with the knowledge that Jesus had forgiven me—past tense, period, next chapter. But the thought had taken hold of me—not as a prosecutor, but as a guide that wanted to set matters right. I understood, though, that it was God and that I couldn't easily chase Him away. He gives not only forgiveness and peace but also requires truth and justice. Thus, was it too much to ask that I offer my apologies to the people I had robbed, cheated, and injured? Offering my excuses was the least I could do, and if it was a matter affecting someone else, then I would say that there should also eventually be monetary restitution in the case of theft.

Knowing the truth is good, but as for myself, it was more painful because it would take me many years to repay all the damage I had done. On my radiant horizon, a dark cloud had appeared, and through this, I felt a bit defeated. For the first time, I prayed very specifically to Jesus for advice.

I said, "Lord Jesus, I don't know how to solve this. Please give me advice."

In the days that followed, a couple of events from my time of addiction came to mind. First, in connection with the many things that I had stolen from a department store, and secondly, with paintings that I had stolen from a landlord. Furthermore, there were a number of people that I felt I owed apologies by means of a letter or a phone call. When I accepted the decision to do this, a load fell off my shoulders.

DEPARTMENT STORE

Nervously, I went with an envelope, filled with a couple of hundred guilders in it, into the department store.

My mother sat in the car outside, waiting for me. The envelope contained a really small amount in comparison with what I had stolen from the store throughout the years. A symbolic amount and I hoped, to be honest, that they would accept it and not demand a more proportional repayment. I didn't know if they would turn me over to the police, but I wasn't concerned about that. Still somewhat nervous, I walked into the ground floor, and to my surprise, soon saw a store detective. Incidentally, you recognize them soon enough if you have an eye for it, but I knew this one, and he knew me. I walked up to him and asked if he could spare a minute.

Surprised and probably a bit curious, he nodded and waited for what I had to say.

"Um, yes," I had trouble in starting. "I'm really sorry for all the stealing I've done here, and I've come to offer my apologies."

The surprise on his face was even greater.

"I also have some money with me for a symbolic repayment," I said hurriedly. I didn't have anything further to say, and I honestly hoped for acceptance.

I felt very small, and the man could undoubtedly see that from my expression because a big smile came over his face. With this reaction, all the tension fell away, and a feeling of friendship sprang into my heart.

"Now, come with me. The others will also want to hear this," he said, slapping me on the shoulders.

"I'm glad that you are taking it this way," I told him.

"We aren't the worst in the world," he answered jokingly. We went through a familiar door for me and came into the office. It was a good hour.

By the time I was outside again, I looked back toward the entrance to the store. I felt liberated and decided to become one of its regular customers.

FLOWER MAN

A while later, I had saved up five hundred guilders to pay a landlord back. I didn't feel good about him. He sold flowers but dabbled in a lot of other things, too, and hung around with a suspicious crowd. I wondered if the flower stall wasn't just a cover-up.

I had no idea how he would react if I admitted that I had taken some paintings. They were expensive paintings, but there was something suspicious about them. They were stored in a place where you don't usually put paintings. He had probably only kept them for someone else and had had problems when they disappeared. Maybe he would demand a large amount from me or even beat me up. Okay, good, I wasn't a scaredy-cat, and I would stand up to him. He was, as always, at his flower stall, saw me coming, and recognized me immediately.

"Do you have a minute?" I asked, meanwhile letting him see the envelope I had with me.

He looked at me with distrust and turned sideways so that he could hear me better.

"The paintings," I started to say.

"Yeah," he interrupted in a loud voice.

"Uh, listen, I've become a believer, and I'm now clean. I want to settle one or two things . . . I have some money for making restitution . . . "

He looked at me questioningly. "Believing and clean—you certainly look better than you did. I thought you had stolen them," he said, now shaking a finger at me menacingly.

"I'm really sorry. I mean it," I replied defensively.

He pointed and asked, "How much is in that envelope?"

"Five hundred," I replied.

He silently thought about it and rubbed his nose. He turned and took a few steps, then turned back and said, "The five hundred guilders is nothing, but okay, okay. You're getting off easy."

"Good of you," I replied as I handed over the envelope.

"Are you really clean?" he asked as he studied me closely.

It turned into a real conversation in which he was genuinely interested. Every time I happen to be in the neighborhood now, I stop by the flower stall, and if he has someone new working for him, he tells them the whole story. We always have a good laugh about it. And when I go, he always says in a stern voice, "And stay clean, you, and watch out."

MY FATHER

After years of not seeing my father, I felt the need to restore our relationship. During my addiction, I never saw him. He did not bother to look up his son to see if he could maybe do something to help him. I blamed him for this and a number of other things from the past. It bothered me more than I had realized.

But God had forgiven me so many things. Who was I to blame someone else? Still, I couldn't just forgive him. Every time I thought about making contact, it turned me off.

I had to pray hard before I could bring myself to see him without blaming and rejecting him. Later, I visited him, and we had a good talk. He is not a believer, and his way of looking at things is not at all like mine, but our relationship now is okay. Sometime later, we spent a day putting down a terrace in his garden. Through working with him, I learned to see another side of him, and I can now say that I love him. I was pleased, in a way, when he introduced me to his neighbor as his son. When he comes to visit, my children sit on their grandfather's lap.

THE FUTURE

By reading the Bible, my former negative ideas of the future became more realistic images, but nevertheless, an image wherein the truth behind the present situation became visible. That the world is crazy, upside down, disturbed, and is going to pieces as the result of sin is true. This self-destructive social structure is nevertheless not the way God originally intended it to be. Injustice rules, but God will interfere in His time. The Bible describes a future scenario about the last struggle, a great oppression like the world has never seen before—enormous environmental problems political and religious dictators that control everything, so that evil powers will have an enormous space in which to operate. The stirring up of the people and the extreme tension will lead to a third world war, and the destructive results of all these things will be so great that if God does not intervene, there will be no survivors of that period.

BUT GOD WILL INTERFERE!

One day, Jesus Christ will demand His Kingdom and will save the world from the oppressive dictatorships and the injustice. He will establish a world-wide peaceful kingdom. Nature will be restored, and all peoples will have their rightful borders. Justice will prevail, and the world's leaders will be devoted servants of their people in His name.

Jerusalem will be the center from which the law will go forth. You can read all about it in the Bible. In the meantime, Christians must learn to live just lives in an unjust world, which is quite a challenge. The Bible speaks extensively about these matters and tells the truth about today as well as the future. For me and many others, it is a stimulus to see this earthly life as a challenge and to do things with God which are both worthy today and in eternity.

As God's co-laborers, we are in a position to help others follow the Way. Unfortunately, many don't want to choose the Way, while others fall by the wayside, following their own path.

That is really something; the central point is not one's own self, but Christ. And yet, it is written, and I have seen it in my own life, "But seek first his kingdom and his righteousness, and all these things will be given to you as well." The Way is for those seeking the truth.

BACK TO THE HAGUE

As I said, after the first miraculous week following my conversion, I was involved in a boat evangelization campaign from the Dordrecht Evangelization. We preached on the streets of small port cities. One evening, in a full boat after I had told my story, I was allowed to pray with a girl who also wanted to be a Christian. She had some personal problems, but when Eef and I visited her some time later, she was still "on the way," as we called it, with Jesus.

Eef and I joined a small mission school three months after my conversion. It was a Bible training year organized by the World Wide Mission, a Hague mission organization which supports hundreds of local ministers, orphanages, food projects, and institutions for the blind in developing countries.

There is also a separate center for drug rehabilitation and a separate program for ex-junkies. As the training was really meant for people who were older and wanted to go into mission work, Eef and I decided to postpone our marriage for a year. That was not so easy for people like us in a relationship, who were used to doing things together immediately.

We realized, nevertheless, that this was good. We needed some education and development. It would also give us time to become mentally strong.

In Zeeland, we were comparatively safe. After a few months, we spent a weekend in The Hague, visiting Eef's family. When we rode through our old neighborhood, we felt a force drawing us in; we almost gave in to it. In the Koningstraat, we suddenly saw a Christian bookstore and decided to have a look around. It proved to be a refuge because the moment we stepped inside, the tension fell away, and we had a fine talk with Henk Bruggeman, who worked there. Strengthened, we left the shop and rushed back to Zeeland. We weren't strong enough yet!

Toward the end of such a studious year, everyone is trying to determine where God wants him/her to go, and although we had received a couple of offers, our desire to go back to The Hague, evangelize, and try to help junkies there was stronger. We could share with them that there was another way, which most of them had never seriously thought about. Now we were strong enough to do this.

We had nothing more than a few clothes and good intentions when we arrived back in The Hague. Once there, we came in contact with Daan Bonte, leader of the Good Shepherd Foundation. We decided to cooperate with his foundation, and they invested money in our activities. We had a great wedding and began with the work, which we have been doing now for more than twelve years. We have never again used drugs.

After we had been busy in The Hague for just over a year, setting up various activities in the field of evangelization and development work, we still received unemployment benefits. When Eef became pregnant, I wanted to get off the dole.

"What should I do?" I asked myself. I had never learned a trade. After looking around the job market, I discovered that there were a significant number of openings in the field of bookkeeping.

I prayed, "Lord, if You're my Employer, You must provide us with money to live on. Otherwise, I'll go into social work, and I can do evangelism in my free time."

In that week, God spoke to me, saying, "In both choices, I'll bless you; you can choose for yourself."

GOD IS A GENTLEMAN

I considered it as a privilege to be chosen to take the path of mission work. Every Christian is a missionary, and every person is equally important, I well understood; but complete independence, also financial, to set up this kind of work I considered to be a blessing. I was influenced by Acts 28:18 and curious how it would all work out.

That month, I filled in my unemployment insurance card with "strange" answers.

"Have you found an employer?"

I wrote, "Yes, Jesus."

"Address of employer?" "The Way."

Undoubtedly, the people at the unemployment insurance agency thought that I had gone crazy because they deposited the usual payment in my bank account that month.

The next month, I didn't send in a card, and the payments ended. We had a circle of friends to whom we sent a newsletter. I had received confirmation of my choice—not just from hearsay, but from God Himself. We had to watch our spending closely, but we never suffered from lack of money. He took care of us. In the meantime, we could go on with our work and do what we had been called to do—moreover, for longer than twelve years full time. Our happiness was complete with the birth of two wonderful children—a boy, and two years later, a girl. What a marvelous miracle it is to see children being born, especially when they're yours.

CHAPTER 18

GLIMPSES OF HELP

My telephone rang, and I heard a familiar voice. Yes, he had a problem. He had taken pity on two junkies by letting them stay at his house because they were homeless. He had done everything for them in the hope that these two men would get clean and get on the right track. He had given them beds in a small bedroom and on the couch in the living room. He lived alone, so he gave them the freedom of his house, except for the privacy of his own bedroom. In the beginning, the two had acted gratefully and had respected his suggestions and advice. But gradually, they became increasingly bolder and even insolent. They continued using drugs. They eventually stopped hiding the fact that they were using.

If he pointed something out to them, they reacted first rebelliously, then later, even threateningly.

"Now," he said, with increasing emotion in his voice, "I don't dare to say anything anymore. They have the key to the front door; and they do exactly what they like, and things are not good. Now I sleep on the couch, and they have the run of the rest of the house! I try to keep things clean, but it is a thankless task."

We had reached the point where he cried more than he spoke, and I understood that it was time for some calming and comforting words.

"Good, good, brother. We are brothers, aren't we? So, you need help. We must see what would be best."

Luke was, as a result of his social work, now a prisoner in his own home. When I thought about this matter, the Bible story about Paradise came to mind.

God gave the use of a beautiful world with everything in it that man could ever need or want. But man turned from thankfulness to misuse of this trust, took over everything, and ruined it. I prayed to God for wisdom in this matter regarding Luke. After I had done that, I experienced a sort of Higher Power come over this situation, and I felt victory. I promised Luke I would help him.

In this state of mind, I visited Luke with the intention of getting these two guys out of his house. To my great surprise, they allowed themselves to be led away with their few belongings, like docile sheep. I asked one of them the address of a member of his family and brought him there. With little trouble, we were rid of him. The other told me in the car that he didn't have any family in the Netherlands. He had a house, though. With surprise, I asked him why he didn't live in his own house. Ironically, it seemed that a dealer had taken it over to use for business. Ed, as he was called, told me that months ago, he had let a dealer sell drugs from his house. Naturally, this was originally a matter of self-interest, as Ed got his daily fix in return. And indeed, these arrangements often last for only a short time.

At a certain time, the dealer took control of the whole situation and made Ed a sort of slave. In these circles, it is not smart to go to the police, and moreover, to do so leads to punishment. Ed decided to leave things as they were and began to wander around. During this time, he met a friendly fellow named Luke. And so, it came about.

"Ya know, drugs destroy all your relationships, and you even cheat people who want to help you."

"Yeah, tell me something new," I said sarcastically.

During this talk with Ed, I realized that he was motivated to begin another kind of life. He was sick to death of the drug life.

My dilemma was what to do with Ed. Of course, I would bring him into contact with a drug center, but you always had the problem of a long waiting period.

"Maybe I can help you kick drugs, but do you have the guts to do it?" I asked him seriously.

He looked at me a bit strangely because he had taken me to be a policeman or someone of that nature. He gave a positive answer, and I thought it worthwhile to try to help him. At the back of our house was a caravan belonging to the Good Shepherd Foundation. I asked permission to let someone stay there temporarily. They approved my request, and Eef and I saw, as the weeks went by, a fine fellow emerge.

Originally, Ed had come from California, and to a certain extent, he was a believer. We were able to help him further, and he became a good friend and brother. After a number of weeks, he went to Amsterdam to follow a program with the organization, "Heil des Voiks." Thereafter, he lived for a couple of years with a group called Pniel. For many years now, Ed has been assistant manager of a supermarket chain.

STREET CORNER WORK

In the soup bus at Central Station in the Hague, I once had a talk with a long-time junkie. I was doing street-corner evangelistic work, and whenever I came there, I saw him but couldn't make contact with him because of his rejecting attitude. He acted in a very asocial and threatening way toward everyone that came near him. I saw that he was saddled with an enormous anger that he had to fight against. He was very violent and had spent years in jail because of this and other things. One afternoon when I met him again in the soup bus, he was suddenly very open with me.

He told me that perhaps I thought he was a skunk, but I would probably be one, too, if I had gone through what he been through. He said that when he was nine years old, he had been sexually abused by three men and that since then, he had decided never to trust anyone and to use force to keep people around him under control. His openness touched me, and my judgment of him changed as a result.

DRUGS ARE A COLD PEOPLE-KILLER

Over the whole world, thousands of people die as a result of drug abuse. Lia, the girl who came to live above us on the Torenstraat, who was also a friend of Eef, was murdered in a dreadful way on the street one cold night. I could add many names to those mentioned in this book who have been directly or indirectly ruined by the use of drugs.

And then the grief and the terrible things that parents, caregivers, brothers, and sisters of addicts have to go through, and which too often goes unmentioned, is impossible to describe. One day, when I had been working for some time with addicts in The Hague, I was interrupted by the telephone in the middle of a talk with two junkies. When I answered, I heard a familiar voice—Ronald, from Amsterdam.

"Yeah, Rem, I don't know how to tell you, but it's about your brother Fred . . . he's dead."

A shock went through me, and I couldn't say anything.

"I . . . I'll call your mother right away, "he stammered. "The police found him with a needle in his arm . . . I'm so sorry Rem."

And he hung up because he was so distraught. A terrible feeling of sorrow filled my heart, and my eyes filled with tears. In a scream, I swore at drugs. Never have I cried with such despair.

I have to go to my mother, I thought. *She'll collapse.*

Was it really true? I couldn't believe it. I had just seen him the week before—Fred, in the market in Amsterdam where he worked. Everyone knew him there, of course. He was always popular. I had even given him a book about the witness of an ex-junkie who, through his belief, had conquered his problems. A few days later, we, the shattered family, could see him lying in a coffin in a mortuary, uncharacteristically still. My own brother, whom I loved so much.

Carrying a cross, we continued our fight against the drug demon.

On the street, we still meet acquaintances from "our" scene who, still so many years later, use drugs and chase after them until they ruin themselves.

SUZANNE

She had fled Hungary because of the strict communist regime. In Budapest, she sniffed glue, and once in the Netherlands, she quickly fell into the life of a junkie.

She was good-looking, displaced, and at the mercy of the street. Used and misused by Tom, Dick, and Harry, she had to work through one blow after the other until she was finally broken. When our team came across her, she was unreachable and thin as a rake. Mentally and physically, she was a wreck. Several times, she came to us, or we met her on the street, but we couldn't do anything with her. A colleague of ours suggested that she come with him, and he would pray with her. She did that but clearly with no result. Disappointed, we had to put her back on the street again.

A few months later, I met her. She looked good and spoke reasonably well in comparison with her gibberish of a couple of months before. Happily surprised, I asked her what had happened. It appeared that after she had prayed with us, she was no longer able to use drugs. A Higher Power had taken her life into His hands. She still wandered around the streets until the police took her to a psychiatric center. After her body was restored, she was declared to be healthy and released.

I asked her, "How is this possible?"

The answer was, "Jesus has done it."

I have seen several miracles, but this surpassed them all. Later, she went to a Christian drug rehabilitation farm. At the time of this writing, she lives back in Hungary again, is married, and has two children.

CHAPTER 19
EASY AS FALLING OFF A ROOF

Was it all as easy as falling off a roof? We discovered that Christian life is not always easy. There are good times and difficult times, just as with most other people. Through the years, we also had the support of Wim and Marianne Wendt from the Fundament Foundation, two of the leaders of the Bible training school with whom we had developed a good relationship.

Good things happened, but we also had our failures. There were very difficult times in our marriage—learning how to bring up our children, developing self-discipline, continuing with what we began, learning to share, doing the pleasant tasks but also the boring ones, persevering in the periods of the daily grind. We received much support and encouragement from fellow Christians, but at certain times, had difficulty in accepting the disappointment in them. We were able to see our own faults and to deal with them. We were overtired and made refreshed, saw sickness and healing, amd even moments of depression so deep that everything seemed like an enormous black hole, but again while still finding sympathy, wonderment, revelation, and conversion. It is great when you see that God puts a propelling force within Christians. Like other people, Christians go through both high and low points, but he/she receives the love, wisdom, power, and strength to overcome them. This overcoming is a life-long learning process. The end goal is fixed, and it is beautiful.

A Christian also receives a propelling force to do something that really helps the great need in the world, and even if this is only for one person, it is worth the effort.

HERNIA

At a certain time, as a result of too much and too heavy lifting, I landed up in bed with a hernia. I didn't want to be operated on, so I lay in bed to rest. I could barely make it to the bathroom because of the pain, and for the first ten weeks, it only got worse. I had paralysis symptoms in my left leg. I felt let down by the Brothers of Christian Meeting that I attended. I asked forgiveness for everything I could think of that I had done wrong. Eef took care of me like an angel.

I asked myself what I had done to deserve this; although, in reality, I had simply done too much lifting. I went into a deep depression and began to hide from people under the blankets. I couldn't look at anyone without crying, and I wished that I were dead. How could this be—having a sweet wife and two wonderful children? But while battling depression, you can't see anything anymore. The only thing I could do was pray to God for help.

My Bible lay next to me, and one night when I couldn't sleep, I opened it to the book of Proverbs—Proverbs 24—"my son." These words were spoken by my heavenly Father Himself! I was deeply touched and felt full of love and the strong sense that He regarded me as His son. I had learned to know Jesus as a Savior, Victor, and Deliverer. Also, as a Friend and a Refuge. He was everything.

I prayed "Father," but I still had to be healed deep down from a feeling of rejection and disbelief.

I'm still busy with the father-son relationship. My earthly experience of this relationship had been extremely limited, but God wanted and worked toward a fullness in the relationship. Up until that time, I had always been too busy for this, and now that I was bedridden, God was using this time for improving the relationship. Although I experienced these thoughts, the following day, a paralyzing blanket of depression still had hold of me. That afternoon, my mother came to visit. I lay under my blankets; when I looked at her, my eyes filled with tears. She suddenly felt my need and came over and stroked my forehead without saying a word. At that very instant, my depression disappeared just like a cloud of smoke in the wind.

Had it not been for the hernia, I would have started dancing; the sun had again broken through the clouds. The following day, I read Isaiah 66:13, "Just as a mother comforts, so will I comfort you!"

I had peace in knowing that the hernia would heal with rest, and indeed, it did happen that way. I spent a total of four months in bed.

In the deepest valley, on the highest mountain, He is near. Through everything, Jesus is there. He is faithful; He is with His people; and therefore, being a Christian is not always easy, but knowing Him brings deep inner peace and joy. It is a peace that cannot be bought or obtained in any other way in this world. He is the Way, the Truth, and the Life. The truth is that we people all need forgiveness, for He did not die for nothing on the cross. He took our sins upon Himself.

We must convert. He then makes us truly free and goes with us along the way. That is what belief is all about—that God wants to have a personal relationship with us. It is a very special relationship; I can genuinely say that it is the most precious thing a person can have.

It is of great importance to know that being a Christian does not mean simply belonging to a church. He doesn't depend on rituals or standard prayers, nor on so-called "great church leaders," regardless of whatever church one belongs to.

It is written, "In His presence is fullness and peace." On the other hand, this belief is not a kind of hobby. God has a plan for everyone's life, and He wants us to follow Him in His truth because the truth sets us free. I have often experienced that if I follow the words of Jesus that are written in the New

Testament of the Bible in all situations, I find freedom and renewal. When we follow Him, we experience a clean and fruitful life that gives satisfaction. He said, and it is written in the Bible, "No one comes to the Father except through me."

We come to the Father through Christ, and this is a relationship based on love. The Bible states that no one can separate us from the love of Christ. We experience difficult times; but Christ is with us, and therefore, we do not despair. Everything in this world is temporary and will disappear. Many people live only for money and possessions, for power or strange desires, and many conflicts are decided through the barrel of a gun or tank.

In each case, demonic powers have a hold on people through sin, and because of this sin, people are prisoners who are swept along from evildoing to even worse—separation from God. All kinds of different powers appear for a time and then are gone. But the words of Christ are forever.

All who sincerely call on Him are saved from slavery and set free. There is a freedom of the spirit, which passes all understanding. In the end, we all stand before the judgment throne of God, bearing both good and bad. And the only good thing is His way—the Way of Life.

SETTING UP THE FOUNDATION "IN DE VRIJHEID" (IN FREEDOM)

Problems arose within our working relations. When people work together, this sometimes happens, but nothing of the human condition is strange to us. Everything works together for the good of Him who loves us (Romans 8:28), even though this is often seen only in hindsight.

In a time of prayer and Bible reading, I read about Isaac. Genesis 26:22 says, "And he moved from there and dug another well and over that they did not quarrel; so he called it Rehoboth, saying: 'For now the Lord has made room for us, and we shall be fruitful in the land.'"

The text became the living word for Eef and me. I had to begin again in a new place and was sure He would bless us. Wasn't I once in the Schiller

Kibbutz in Rehoboth in Israel? Christ is the Source of life, and He brought us to freedom. I had to establish a new foundation, and it became Foundation for Freedom, freely translated and derived from the Hebrew word "Rehoboth" or "Rechobot."

A number of people were kicking the drug habit in our home, but our children were becoming older, too, so we had the desire to set up a center. We had enthusiasm and no money. But we most definitely had faith. We were convinced that God would provide the means that were needed to do the work.

Oh, how surprisingly God works. Much sooner than we had expected, this desire was heard. A wealthy business couple, people who had been Christians for just a few years, crossed our path.

They "offered" an amount that was an in-between deal, or so they called it. With this amount in mind, we went with these people to look for, and actually found, a nice house for sale that met our requirements. This was ironic because it was owned by a former club owner, the club being one that I had regularly gone to when I was a user. In the attic room, while we were looking at the house, we prayed to God, "Lord, if this is the building, then let this be the possession of the foundation for Your work."

When we talked with the owner and told him what we wanted to use the house for, he was very enthusiastic and said that he wanted to sell it to us because he, too, had seen enough misery as a result of drugs.

His lawyer then came into the room with the announcement that he had just sold the house to someone who had looked at the house before we did.

We left, but we still had hope in our hearts. That same evening, the owner of the building called to say that he had been able to avert the sale on the grounds of a transfer clause and that he would be glad to sell it to us.

"And," he said jovially, "you can have it for ten thousand guilders less!"

You can imagine how we celebrated that evening. At that time, we had been off drugs for ten years.

Now, the center has been operating for some years, and although it demands an enormous amount of energy and effort to keep it all running smoothly, it is worth twice the effort.

Scores of alcohol, drugs, and gambling addicts have made a fresh start from the center In de Vrijheid (In Freedom) and have gone on to lead new and fruitful lives.

EXPANSION OF THE INTAKE CAPACITY

Three years after the opening of the center in The Hague, there came an expansion of the work. We discovered an evangelical organization for alcohol, drugs, and gambling addicts that had centers throughout Sweden. We visited one of these centers, which is situated on a large piece of land with a capacity for twenty guests. Several married couples live there and operate the center. In the garden, there was enough room for both gardening and sports activities.

I stood in that garden and took a deep breath. "Lord, it would be great to have something like this for our foundation, In de Vrijheid in The Hague."

Back in The Hague, we had a visitor at our door. Annemarie was a girl who, earlier in the year, had managed to kick her drug habit with us and had gone on to a follow-up center. She needed a roof over her head. It appeared that she had left the intake house. After some discussion, Eef and I went to Zeeland to the intake center to pick up Annemarie's clothes.

While we were there, we had a talk with the married couple who ran the center. It seemed that they had been looking for replacements to run the center for more than eighteen months because they were no longer able to continue the work since they were in their sixties. After approaching various organizations and individuals about this but leaving with no success, they had finally made an agreement with the alderman of the municipality to sell the building. This, however, would be completely opposite to their desire that the center should continue to be used for evangelical purposes.

We were shown around the house and realized that it would be very useful for the intake work that we were doing in The Hague. The building was in perfect condition. We told them about our work, and soon, the couple saw in us their possible successors. Eef and I were amazed at this sudden possibility to expand.

The extensive area, both inside the building and the garden around it, inspired such a feeling of breathing space that I couldn't help thinking back to my prayer in the garden in the center in Sweden.

That week, we prayed about it, and together, with the members of the board, we went to look it over once again. Finally, we were all in agreement, and the board unanimously voted for this center. In the new center, there is room for a maximum of twenty-five guests.

My hope is that you, too, will learn to live with Him. It all begins with prayer. Pray sincerely to Christ and follow his directions. You will then find help. Then, give yourself a few years to become spiritually strong. Don't think you will necessarily have to work with addicts or do other complicated work. God has different plans for different people, but you can only discover this when you walk in His Way. And you will surely come to know that He is the living God, through Whom nothing is impossible!

Wishing you Strength and Blessings,
Remko E. Jorritsma

APPENDIX

If you want information about Christian Intake Centers, send a card to:

Stichting In de Vrijheid

Postbus 82

4420 AC, Kapelle, Nederland

RECOMMENDED BOOKS

Above all other books, I recommend reading the Bible, which was written by forty writers over a period of about fifteen hundred years. These writers were inspired by God. The Bible is the most translated and sold book in the world. Millions of people have found the Source of Life through reading it. Buy it in a present-day language version that is easy to read, but we also recommend that you read it in the New International Version (NIV).

I would like to recommend the following books, which will help you see your innermost problems and how to live with them and work through them:

- *Walls of My Heart* by Dr. Bruce Thomson
- *Freed to Be Free* by Tom Marshall
- *The Art of Parental Love* by Dr. Ross Campbell

SURVEY OF CAUSES OF ADDICTION

Knowing the causes of a problem is a great help in seeking solutions. To know is to understand. Trying to get a handle on things is a necessary and continual activity for every person. I personally think that trying to get an understanding in all areas of life is a task for everyone. It is also an absorbing pursuit and one that has a promise—"seek and ye shall find."

The most important starting point for this is to look for the truth. There is much to say about this in general, but we will limit ourselves on this subject.

Eef and I have spent more than twelve years now working with addicts. Through our own addiction background, the ability to put ourselves in their shoes is a plus point in comparison to workers who do not have this background. Such a background is, however, not at all essential in order to do this work. But it does help. One of the conditions for an ex-addict is that the addiction has really been conquered and that falling back into it is out of the question. Therefore, it is much better for some ex-addicts to stay as far away as possible from care-giving and to look for work in some other field.

After missionary school, I took a lot of courses and did a great deal of self-study to improve myself. I also had work experience periods in various intake centers, so that I could see how they worked. As a result of all these things, I became curious about what, in general, was the reason that people became addicted to drugs. I began my own research. Stories told by many addicts who I knew personally and questions asked to guests in our center, who were there to kick the habit, gave me the opportunity to get what I considered to be a realistic picture. What I discovered was that the main reasons were both shocking and confrontational but, in hindsight, logical.

The reasons for becoming addicted mentioned here below could also be listed as reasons for going off the track in general. While the word "addiction" brings to mind, in the first place, alcohol, drugs, and gambling, it is clear that many more people are addicted to other things that are more socially acceptable and, at first sight, less harmful.

Many addictions, although less harmful economically, are nevertheless of great cost to society. A typical Western way of going off the tracks is being a workaholic. The driving force behind this can be a career, a position, money, or material self-satisfaction. Addiction is an appetite that is insatiable and all demanding (i.e. addiction to power, lust, food, computers, TV, etc.). The addiction is characterized by the fact that it must be constantly repeated; the same circle must be followed, even if it leads to death. For the workaholic, this can be caused by a heart attack. The reasons for drug addiction mentioned here can just as well pertain to going off the track in general.

When we think about going astray, this can be applicable to whole societies and groups in a world that has become an impossible mess.

"Back to basics" should be the motto of the care-giver. These care-givers should first clean up their own acts and return to the basics themselves. But what are these basics?

In any event, I became a teetotaler when an alcoholic asked me to help him. An alcoholic must make the radical but necessary choice never again to have an alcoholic drink, not even one beer, regardless of circumstances. I should have a stable marriage in order to help someone with marital problems. I should be close to my children to ensure that they are happy and that they develop in a balanced way. That means time and effort for my wife and me, but how great is the result? If all goes well, then I can give parents good advice on this subject.

I am always shocked when a care-giver or administrator has a firm conviction about relationships, while he or she changes partners every couple of years. I have trouble with people who have a lot to say about upbringing when their relationship with their own children is bad. These are people who tell others what to do when their own lives are messy and empty.

Word with deed is strength. Word without deed is empty, and empty are the admonitions of a parent who doesn't have a real concern for his/her child.

The causes of addiction certainly lie mostly in the field of relationships, but not always. For example, an important cause is very simple—availability.

If you can't obtain something, it can't be used. That is simple. Someone who wants to buy drugs cannot be stopped. Demand plus money leads to supply. Some people go to great lengths. Look at the trade in human organs;

there are even murders committed for this purpose. Commercial interest is often the motive for the offer of drugs. When drugs first came, they were forced on young people by the pushers. In the sixties and seventies, the pushers were found near the school grounds and in the discotheques and youth centers to actively recruit new users. Pop groups pushed drugs as being able to expand the mind and make it more innovative. In the beginning, drugs were used by small groups, which together formed a sort of sub-culture.

Society was opposed to drug use. Progressive youth media, the pop culture, and commercial interests introduced the terms "soft drugs" and "hard drugs" and convinced the ill-informed policymakers and the public of the harmlessness of and the "expanding" nature of "soft drugs" ("soft drugs" being cannabis products by the names of hashish, marijuana, grass, and skunk).

The pro-drugs lobby was successful, as the cannabis product drugs have, since 1976, been declared "legal" by way of the drug toleration policy. It is even the case that certain subsidized youth centers have an appointed house dealer. In this way, the government cooperates in the spread of drugs. The result of the drug toleration policy is, as I see it, that many more people began to be users. From this policy, the way was made free for commercial "coffee shops," of which there are now fifteen hundred in the Netherlands.

After several decades of the drug toleration policy, the number of cannabis product users in the Netherlands has enormously increased. There are now more than eight hundred thousand cannabis users. There are also about the same number of problem drinkers in this country, but this total has developed over a long period of time. The same number of drug users has come about in less than thirty years, and it is estimated that total users will increase threefold in the coming two decades!

Now that the scale of the problem is becoming known, we see parents and citizens protesting because of the nuisance it causes. In families, the suffering caused by drugs and alcohol use is enormous.

The damage from cannabis use is highly underrated (see our flyer "Soft Drugs Soft"). Our foundation is, therefore, against any form of toleration policy. This is based purely on the fact that availability alone is one of the causes of addiction and getting off track. We plead for prosecution of every kind of trade. Note that the trade, not the drug users, should be prosecuted, as is the case in the United States. Any kind of trade and offer of drugs should be forbidden and legally dealt with.

As I have said, anyone who wants to use drugs will certainly be able to get a hold of them, but by tolerating the sale of drugs, the government helps with the spread of drug use. Moreover, the government gives a false signal that the tolerated drugs are not dangerous.

Many young people who can easily obtain drugs will quickly start experimenting with them. A certain number of them will continue to use and will experience the results. A given percentage of the cannabis users will switch over to the so-called "hard drugs."

It is a well-known fact that, by far, most hard drug users began with cannabis products. Moreover, it is paradoxical that, on the one hand, a government spends millions to get users "clean" in withdrawal centers and on the other hand, allows hundreds of dealing addresses to function in the form of "coffee shops" (the term for cannabis businesses in the Netherlands).

The circulation of drugs also occurs among young people. In a group, a joint is suddenly passed around, and as a youth, it is very difficult to resist group pressure by saying no. Those who can manage to do that have real character.

In nightclubs and at house parties, many different drugs are on offer and freely used. People are tempted in all kinds of ways to "try it just once" or to "experiment." The Bible teaches us, in Ephesians 6, that we must resist the temptation of the devil. For tempting people is of the devil and worse than sinning itself. Young Christian people must also be strong in the power of the Lord to be able to withstand temptation. It is possible: "Resist the devil, and he will flee from you" (James 4:7).

The temptation lasts but a short time, and with victory comes happiness. Then there is room for healthy activities—good relationships, sports and hobbies, work and studies.

If there is transgression, there is forgiveness for those who humble themselves, but there is a disastrous road ahead for those who slip away.

In addition to availability, the lack of the positive presence of a father (parent, care-giver) is the main cause of drug addiction. Lack of the positive presence of the father in the life of a child, and especially of sons, was one of the most important causes that came out of my survey. At first, this surprised me because I had expected it to be the consumer (throwaway) society, which I find so disastrous for the human spirit. The absence of the father is often due to divorce, and divorce is becoming more and more prevalent, resulting in children no longer getting the attention that they should receive. The breakup of a marriage has a negative effect in many ways on the psychological development of a child.

In many cases, the father's career, which often takes up all his time, is the culprit. In our Western society, what you do defines who you are; a person is what he produces. Someone's worth is determined by what he does, accomplishes, earns, or makes. How people function in regard to relationships is of secondary importance. Not how another has reached what he has but only that he has reached it is what is considered to be important. The excuse that bread has to be put on the table is an easy one. Often what is meant by "bread" is a nice home, a car, status, competitive position, rank, prestige, hobbies, and the like.

Of course, members of a family do enjoy this material prosperity. However, it is certainly not their main need. It can also be that a father's time is completely taken up because he can't say no to his employer.

Parents need to be helped to see that good relationships are more important than anything else and thus learn to communicate well with others and rediscover how great being with people can be.

LACK OF ATTENTION.

In the house but too busy watching TV or at home but mindlessly reading the paper. There but busy with his own hobbies. At home but too busy with his thoughts. Far away. Father is home but not home. No focused attention, no having fun or helping a child with his homework or going with him to a sports game. A child wants to be seen, to get attention, to be cuddled, to hear stories, to see that he or she is important to the parents. In addition to my work, I wanted to start a go-cart club for children aged six to twelve. I organized routes, and the children on the street loved it.

But I noticed that the children liked it better if there was some adult leadership. The usual pecking order among the children was thereby avoided, and the younger children felt safer. I noticed that there were hardly ever any parents to play with the children or to help organize activities. The children were left to their own devices. Obviously, the parents did not take time to be actively involved with their children.

The problems caused by the absence of parents (latch-key children) are well-known, and an enormous emotional need often develops as a result.

LIVING IN A RESIDENTIAL HOME

Many addicts come from residential homes. There is, of course, care in these places, but it can never equal that of parental home care. When the special love and care of parents is absent, this in itself is damaging for a child. Moreover, in these residential homes, there is often a group mentality whereby the law of the strongest rules.

While working in rehabilitation, I have been confronted with boys in their teens who have fallen into the hands of homosexuals and pedophiles, not because these boys had homosexual tendencies, but simply because they longed for some fatherly warmth. Homosexuals and pedophiles often take advantage of this longing. The same reason can explain the behavior of girls who get involved with much older men.

I read somewhere that nothing can be more satisfactory than to see your children develop into emotionally mature people. I firmly believe this. One of the first questions I ask when I meet older people is if they have any children. The knowledge of having been caring parents leads to great contentment. To meet grandchildren who have grown up in a good family and are happy people is one of the great riches in life. Life, after all, is all about relationships and not possessions. Anyone with a lot of broken relationships has, in the end, nothing.

Does this mean that the cause of addiction always lies with the parents? Absolutely not. There are of course, other reasons, a few of which are mentioned below.

One reason is a negative view of the future (environmental pollution, world events, war, recession, etc.). I could determine this clearly with regard to myself. The negative view of the future that I had on the basis of data concerning environmental developments was sufficient for me to decide not to spend too much time on laying foundations to provide for important future needs, for example, a full-time job, a pension, or other such things.

The other side of the coin was that in no way did I wish the following generation to have the misery that they would face in view of the sick environment, and therefore, I would ensure that, as far as I was concerned, there would be no next generation. I didn't want any children.

The only alternative was to take advantage of each day, as long as there was a day. Working was only a means of earning money, and money provided the possibility to take advantage of all sorts of pleasures—going out, drinking, having many girlfriends, taking trips, and doing drugs—everything that could make life pleasant and exciting. It had to be instant, right now and direct. Whether the means were dangerous or not, it didn't matter, for tomorrow may never come. Of course, this philosophy is in conflict with actual needs—a house, rest, certainty and safety, as well as a conscience and the will to survive. The philosophy of luxury does not allow for permanent relationships either.

Therefore, the pain of broken relationships often comes as an unnecessary consequence to keep one company.

Anyone who seeks only after pleasure and the kicks in life naturally experiences their painful disadvantages. From personal experience, I found that the very things that actually gave pleasure, in fact, began ruling my life. Drinking, drugs, free sex, gambling, overeating, pills, etc.—habits that grew from little puppies into enormous dogs, which could hardly be controlled. Being attacked by such a vicious dog can make you suddenly aware of your addictive situation and the need to get free of it; but that is not easy.

Many become discouraged because of unsuccessful attempts and reach the point where they just give up the fight. A defeated spirit makes the bones wither. A deathly and empty existence is all that remains. Emptiness, unemployment, loneliness, and lack of spirituality, idealism, purpose, and self-discipline.

Reasons for going off the track, like addiction, are often conclusions that every thinking person comes to and are confirmed by investigation. It is also clear that one cause overlaps another and that many different causes can be present with an addict. In care-giving with ex-addicts, and also ex-prisoners or the parole service, the so-called re-entry into society is of great importance. Rightly so, it is said that emptiness is the devil's pillow. A purposeful use of time is encouraged by the necessary motivating stimulants in the form of salary and promotion possibilities.

That eighty percent of the ex-prisoners fall back into their old patterns of living is a well-known fact. This is also true for ex-addicts who, after a drug-free period, try to acclimate themselves back into society. In the beginning, the ex-junkie is well-motivated and tries to stay clean and make a whole new start in life. But work is not easy to find, especially interesting work. In order to get the necessary professional knowledge, self-discipline and good study habits are needed, which are often lacking in the ex-junkie who has to kill time hanging around in the city. It won't be long before he is addicted again.

I have seen that even many young people who have a reasonable job and are integrated into society start using drugs on the weekends.

The linking up of ex-junkies with clean people is often difficult. In the scene, the drug users' world, people know each other and have friends and speak the same language. People visit one another to score and use drugs. The drug is something which they have in common, and it creates a bond.

Using drugs together gives a certain feeling of belonging. It's more attractive to become addicted together than to be clean alone in one's room. In addition to these things, we can feel the spiritual needs of people. It is not possible to fill a spiritual vacuum just by material and social means. Man does not live by bread alone.

TRAUMATIC EXPERIENCES

A trauma can result from an incident—for example, a violent robbery, rape, war, violence, or other shocking occurrences. A trauma, then, results from a shock. It can also result from a series of unnatural experiences or some other course of events, such as a dominating, unapproachable father who develops a kind of macho relationship with his son; a son who is controlled by beating; a girl who is sexually abused; a child who is held back; a child who is always teased or is misused as a work slave; a child on which too high demands are made; a child who is over-indulged; a child who can't meet the expectations of his parents and is thereby ignored by those caring for him.

There are many causes that can be listed for psychic damage. Helping people work through a trauma requires good insight, understanding, and patience. Trauma leads to all kinds of fears, frustration, anger, shame, and false guilt feelings. Of course, these feelings influence behavior and lifestyle.

A certain group will try to deaden the inner pain caused by the trauma with drugs. These people can be found in all groups, from silent drinkers to violent junkies and criminals. I know a junkie pimp, an unfeeling figure, who was sexually abused by men when he was a boy; a junkie who sought anesthetics because he became an incurable cripple when he was sixteen; a dealer who committed two murders in his dealer circle, who grew up with the torture weapon of his father's belt. I know many, many examples of addicts for whom the root cause has been trauma.

A caregiver must have insight and understanding for certain kinds of behavior in order to understand the depth of certain addiction causes or to minimize them. On the other hand, criminal behavior cannot be justified simply because it is caused by a trauma; each person is responsible for his or her own actions.

That is an eternal law. God, however, can and will give mercy and healing to those suffering from trauma. There is much to say about the way in which He will do it. The Bible says that God's power is to help in accordance with His Gospel. In other words, in His own way. His way is the best way, and the Bible gives advice on all subjects. In the "Lord's Prayer," Jesus teaches praying but also proclaims spiritual truths that, when applied, will lead to the desired healing. I know women who have forgiven those who committed incest with them; there are people who have experienced unjustified violence and who have wrestled with and won, through Jesus, over the hate that was in their hearts against those who had harmed them. I have enormous respect for such people. Christ Himself said, when He suffered as an innocent man nailed to the cross, "Father, forgive them, for they know not what they do."

For more information about

Remko Jorritsma

and

Off the Streets and On the Way

please visit:

www.facebook.com/stichting.indevrijheid.9

For more information about
AMBASSADOR INTERNATIONAL
please visit:

www.ambassador-international.com
@AmbassadorIntl
www.facebook.com/AmbassadorIntl

*Thank you for reading this book. Please consider leaving us a
review on your social media, favorite retailer's website,
Goodreads or Bookbub, or our website.*

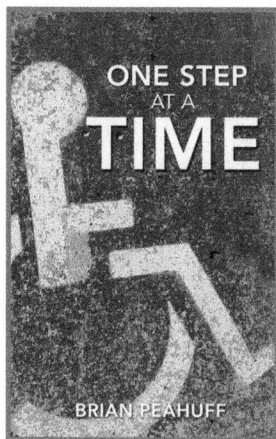

After a car accident left him paralyzed at the age of eighteen, Brian Peahuff thought he was destined to live a hopeless and helpless life. But God had other plans for Brian. *One Step at a Time* begins with Brian's last high school football game in 1990 and chronicles all the ups-and-downs of the next twenty-six years. It's a story of tragedy, a story of determination and perseverance, a story about willpower and never giving up, and then an unexpected love story.

Step 13 is the true story of how one man struggled with alcohol addiction and how God used this life to bring glory to Himself. Jim Brissey opens his heart and honestly portrays his day-to-day struggle to give up his "good friend, Buzz." As he shares his own struggles to overcome alcohol and worship God to the fullest, Jim testifies that God can, indeed, use anyone to bring others to Him.

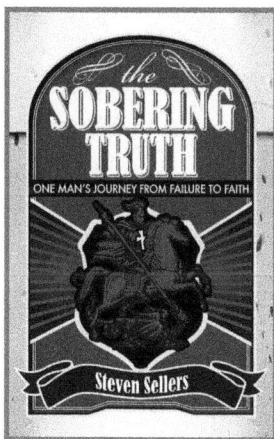

Steven Sellers was at the bottom of his bottle . . . literally. *The Sobering Truth* follows Steven to his breakdown, physically and spiritually. It addresses life in treatment both in and out of the hospital and the ever present threat of relapse. This story describes how the Addict can move beyond sobriety and learns how to embrace life in recovery; how to fill the hollow void that the ravenous Beast left in its place. Written for those who may be battling the Beast in their own lives, or for the family members desperate to understand their loved one, The Sobering Truth reveals insight about the inner workings of the Addict and most importantly, hope for a God-directed recovery.

www.ingramcontent.com/pod-product-compliance
Lightning Source LLC
Chambersburg PA
CBHW071443090426
42737CB00011B/1758

9 781649 602114